CRITICAL GEOGRAPHIES OF EDUCATION

Critical Geographies of Education: Space, Place, and Curriculum Inquiry is an attempt to take space seriously in thinking about school, schooling, and the place of education in larger society. In recent years spatial terms have emerged and proliferated in academic circles, finding application in several disciplines extending beyond formal geography. Critical Geography, a reconceptualization of the field of geography rather than a new discipline itself, has been theoretically considered and practically applied in many other disciplines, mostly represented by what is collectively called social theory (i.e., anthropology, sociology, cultural studies, political science, and literature). The goal of this volume is to explore how the application of the ideas and practices of Critical Geography to educational theory in general and curriculum theorizing in specific might point to new trajectories for analysis and inquiry.

This volume provides a grounding introduction to the field of Critical Geography, making connections to the significant implications it has for education, and by providing illustrations of its application to specific educational situations (i.e., schools, classrooms, and communities). Presented as an intellectual geography that traces how spatial analysis can be useful in curriculum theorizing, social foundations of education, and educational research, the book surveys a range of issues including social justice and racial equity in schools, educational reform, internationalization of the curriculum, and how schools are placed within the larger social fabric.

Robert J. Helfenbein is Associate Dean for Research and Faculty Affairs and Professor of Curriculum Studies in the Tift College of Education at Mercer University. His current research interests include curriculum theorizing in urban contexts, cultural studies of education, and the impact of globalization on the lived experience of schools.

CRITICAL GEOGRAPHIES OF EDUCATION

Space, Place, and Curriculum Inquiry

Robert J. Helfenbein

Routledge
Taylor & Francis Group

NEW YORK AND LONDON

First published 2021
by Routledge
605 Third Avenue, New York, NY 10158

and by Routledge
2 Park Square, Milton Park, Abingdon, Oxon, OX14 4RN

Routledge is an imprint of the Taylor & Francis Group, an informa business

Library of Congress Cataloging-in-Publication Data
Names: Helfenbein, Robert J., author.
Title: Critical geographies of education : space, place, and curriculum
inquiry / Robert J. Helfenbein.
Description: New York, N.Y. : Routledge, 2021. | Includes bibliographical
references.
Identifiers: LCCN 2020056126 (print) | LCCN 2020056127 (ebook) | ISBN
9781032014333 (hardback) | ISBN 9780367407797 (paperback) | ISBN
9781003178590 (ebook)
Subjects: LCSH: Educational planning--Social aspects. | Curriculum
planning--Social aspects. | Spatial behavior.
Classification: LCC LB2806 .H43 2021 (print) | LCC LB2806 (ebook) | DDC
371.2/07--dc23
LC record available at https://lccn.loc.gov/2020056126
LC ebook record available at https://lccn.loc.gov/2020056127

ISBN: 978-1-032-01433-3 (hbk)
ISBN: 978-0-367-40779-7 (pbk)
ISBN: 978-1-003-17859-0 (ebk)

Typeset in Bembo
by SPi Global, India

This book is dedicated to all the students and educators that I have learned so much from over the years and spaces of my life. Words are not enough.

CONTENTS

MAPS

Note

1 The data shown on these maps were classified using the Natural Breaks/Jenks method. The reason why the three maps have different classes was to accentuate the differences in the racial makeup in these areas, as all three have unique demographic characteristics. All new maps created by Ryan Leighton (rleighton917@gmail.com).

PREFACE

An Intellectual Geography

I write this preface in the Fall of 2020, a year that will not be soon forgotten as the world struggled with the Covid-19 virus and what was often a bumbling political response. To varying degrees, people have been in social isolation, or quarantine, or at least in masks and social distancing; some in the United States, of course, denied it was happening at all and didn't do any of those things. But this is a book about geography and it is striking how, in this time of global pandemic, we look at maps everyday: maps of infection, maps of mortality, maps of school closures, and maps of political efforts at containment. It is difficult not to see that the central lesson here is one of relationality, how our actions impact other people; we are in relation. Regardless of our political positions, ardent ideological stances, or susceptibility to propaganda, one way or another, the virus points to a relational geography as spaces are always, already interconnected.

2020 and the nation also saw the death of George Floyd at the hands of Minneapolis police, sparking national protests, yet again, that continued throughout the year. Tracing back to Ferguson, Missouri activists aligned with the Movement for Black Lives claimed spaces public and private in the hopes of bringing new power to the longstanding struggle of racial justice in the United States. Social protest has always historically had a spatial component, be it demanding access to spaces previously denied or simply finding spaces where visibility and attention to certain issues cannot be avoided. Of course, these moves often inspire countermeasures where spaces are defended, borders reinforced, and transgression is met with violence. Occupy Wall Street, Standing Rock, and Tahir Square during the so-called Arab Spring brought the spatiality of social protest movements to the foreground, quite literally claiming and occupying space for extended periods; these lessons and tactics carried forward into the protest movements of 2020. Confederate Monuments too are about the appropriateness of marking spaces, using spaces to teach people things, and what it means to reject those lessons. But if we tighten the scale, we also see race and space intertwined in the killing by police of Breonna Taylor in her own home, of Ahmaud Arbery and Trayvon Martin killed by white men allegedly protecting property, and children in cages at our southern borders. We could similarly document the ways in which women, LGBTQ+ folk, those living in poverty, and the disability community all struggle with issues of space and place. This is a meager listing of what is a long, sad, historical record but one that points to what can be at stake in taking space seriously and is also an indelible part of the fabric of a year.

Since the early 2000s I have been writing about Critical Geography and how it might be useful in curriculum theorizing, educational research, and foundations of education. Merging with another interest in cultural studies via Birmingham, I focused on spatial thinking that privileged the material aspects of space as part of an inquiry that saw space and the people within it as mutually constitutive. In other words, I wanted to talk about space and place beyond the merely discursive. Others in educational theorizing have taken up spatial metaphors in interesting and generative ways but my usage of those discursive tools has been intended to point to *a material geography* of physical spaces. This doesn't make one project wrong and one right but it does point to difference in approach and potentially different possibilities for analysis. As what I hope gets laid out in the pages that follow, I want to suggest, and suggest again, that place matters, that taking space seriously matters, and that curriculum matters. What I have tried to weave together here is that simple argument and all the incomplete complexities that go into it.

I'm calling this book an intellectual geography as my intent is to track the development of the ideas around a critical geography of education as developing over space just as much as developing over time. After laying out a theoretical framework, the chapters of the book trace my journey from dissertation research to current research projects and hope to show how ideas built upon one another as I traveled from place to place. Each chapter begins with a vignette, told in an informal voice, describing the material, physical experience of moving to new places as each one brought new things to light and added nuance to an analysis of contemporary education. The hope here lies in showing ideas in movement, emergent and not yet done. Notable in thinking about this assemblage of ideas as a whole is the recognition of how much more explicit race becomes as part of the inquiry and part of the analysis. Not to say that it wasn't always there—segregation in education looms large in our history and is, by definition, spatial—but as ideas and inquiries formed along the way, race, anti-blackness, the postcolonial, and white supremacy sharpened in analytic relief. Especially in US contexts, race and space are inextricably intertwined. As my journey gets mapped here, a racial critique not only comes into clearer focus but becomes all the more urgent as we try to understand the spaces we find ourselves in.

1

CRITICAL GEOGRAPHY AND EDUCATION

An Introduction

This intellectual geography begins at Appalachian State University in a Master's seminar in Geography. Here, I was introduced to the idea of marxist (the small "m" was intentional) and feminist geography. I simply hadn't thought about how a theoretical frame might impact the work of geographers, but the idea that maps had authors, biases, and political goals didn't take long to sink in—my paper in that class was on the Zapatistas and the claim that they were the first postmodern revolution. What was already a deep interest in history became a much more socio-spatial view—one that began to ask questions about the entanglements of history, geography, and the social. I can clearly remember that classroom, that place; I remember it with an embodied feeling that something new was happening, my thinking was changing and it was exciting. The Geography Department had its own floor and the graduate students had their own space, a shared office where late-night papers were written and good Costa Rican coffee was consumed in quantity (beans were brought back every year from a study abroad program). Other students were obsessed with the new technology, Geographic Information Systems, while others dug deep into the study of national hazards, notably hurricanes as we were in North Carolina, and I started to look for linkages between culture and place, history and spatial distribution, and how space became place or, in other words, what was the role of place in how people make sense of the world.

I came down from the mountains of North Carolina and back to the city of Raleigh to teach high school, a dramatic change in scene and professional responsibility but also a homecoming of sorts (I grew up in Raleigh) that carried with it all the good and bad of those memories. Places are haunted with memory. In my social studies classroom, I was only vaguely aware of how much space and place I was putting into my courses; I'm not sure how many World Civ teachers spend significant time on the Roman Climatic Optimum to explain the rise and fall of ancient Rome. But I did start to raise some spatial questions in that role of high school teacher as some fellow critical teachers and I began to think deeply about equity and opportunity at our school. For example, why were the special education classrooms so far from the front door? How did the tracking of students within the school map onto these hallways and how were those policies raced and classed? Why was my classroom a safe space for kids that didn't quite fit in, filled at lunch time with punk kids, queer kids, hip-hop kids?

After several years of teaching, I travelled down the road to Chapel Hill and began doctoral work in Culture, Curriculum, and Change (RIP). There I found a place both familiar (as I did undergraduate study there) and strange (I was not longer 20 years old) as well as two fields of study, Cultural Studies of Education and Curriculum Theory, that would give me language for what I felt in my gut about teaching and schools. Here is where I found scholars taking up what would be called Critical Geography.

> The great obsession of the nineteenth century was, as we know, history: the present epoch will perhaps be above all the epoch of space. We are in the epoch of simultaneity: we are in the epoch of juxtaposition, the epoch of the near and far, of the side-by-side, of the dispersed. We are at a moment, I believe, when our experience of the world is less that of a long life developing through time than that of a network that connects points and intersects with its own skein.
>
> (Foucault & Miskowiec, 1986, p. 22)

To begin to explore critical geographies of education we will start where I did in my doctoral study: digging deep into critical theories of society, culture, processes of meaning-making, and curriculum as an entrée into new understandings of the place called school. To say that social theory now questions much of what was once considered neutral or natural in knowledge production and ways of knowing would be an understatement. In contemporary social theory, a variety of critical discourses—including but not limited to postmodernism, poststructuralism, feminism, postcolonialism, decolonialism, queer theory, affect theory, new materialisms, and posthumanism—have been bringing issues of power, language, positionality, subjectivity, affect, and voice to the fore. These discourses challenge disciplinary claims to universality, transparency, objectivity, and truth, critically examining those concepts instead as social constructions that serve to both reinforce and advance particular understandings about the world. Curriculum theory and cultural studies of education are deeply impacted by these new directions in thinking through issues of education, the broader social world, and how we make meaning in/of the world.

Scholars in the discipline of geography have, in various ways, engaged such challenges around being/knowing/doing.[1] This text represents an attempt to further explicate how such engagements have already and might continue to bridge spatial and education theorizing. Research informed by Critical Geography— both empirical and theoretical—opens up possibilities for re-thinking the object, nature, and substance of educational research by providing another entrée into questioning the givenness of the world, the knowable transparency of language, and the nature of power and its entanglement with the subjects that it acts upon (see Weedon, 1999). This work suggests new avenues for research in curriculum theory and cultural studies of education that address some of the pertinent—and I would argue more interesting—critical issues engaged by geographers and social theorists as a result of the above challenges.

This book—and, for that matter the decades of work it compiles—takes up the questions of what might it mean for educational theorist to "take space seriously" and what then would it mean to theorize curriculum as a spatial text? The eponymous text *Understanding Curriculum: An Introduction to the Study of Historical and Contemporary Curriculum Discourses* (Pinar, Reynolds, Slattery, & Taubman, 1995) does not include a section on thinking curriculum spatially. Today, however, this addition could be done. Cognitive mapping, curriculum mapping, and meaning maps are but a few examples of spatial terms making their way into curriculum discourse. But what I offer here—what elsewhere I have called "taking space seriously" (Helfenbein 2011a)—implies more substantive shifts in the ways scholars look at the lived experience of schools. Educational research tends to consider classrooms and schools as bounded spaces; tightly constrained, these limits allow for simpler analysis and a neater path toward conclusions. However, to better understand the complexity of educative spaces, a critical geography approach acknowledges that sociomaterial systems like schools are bound in a "tangled web of practices." These practices include communities, sedimented histories, economic and cultural contexts, connections to multiple layers of government, as well as identities, ideologies, and affects ; Nespor, 1997; Tyack & Cuban, 1995). Requiring multiple levels of analysis, the scalar approach of Critical Geography opens up inquiry into learning, teaching, and curriculum in educative spaces to a greater complexity.

Beginning with the theoretical underpinnings, we begin this intellectual geography with definitions and key concepts that characterize a critical approach to spatial analysis and move toward questions related to geography as curriculum. The implications of taking space seriously then reverberate through questions not only of curriculum theorizing but also into questions of methodology and inquiry itself. Much like a scalar geography, the intention is to pull in and out in terms of focus, moving from the local to the global and back again in the hope of seeing things in relation, in process, and in intra-action[2].

Critical Geography: A Theoretical Framework

> Geography, as we know, is always about knowledge.
> -Katherine McKittrick, Demonic Grounds

To make geography *critical*, scholars began by critiquing the failings of positivism and took up the tools of existentialism and phenomenology. Starting to infuse questions of identity, difference, and new conceptions of the subject into spatial analysis (see Tuan, 1977), influences from feminist and Marxist thinkers helped new spatial questions to emerge. As scholars began to see gendered, classed, and raced geographies, they necessarily infused their work with theories of both power and agency. An earlier scholarly struggle between deterministic emphases on the local or the global was slowly chipped away, a shift reflected in other disciplines. As these concerns and other epistemologies moved through the "posts," a small group of geographers influenced by the work of Birmingham cultural studies began to form a body of work that could be recognized as Critical Geography. Refusing to think in terms of determinism, or the "either, or" of traditional spatial analysis and theorizing, Critical Geography rather insists on what I call the "yes, and." This is similar to what has been called the "next moment" in curriculum theorizing (Malewski, 2010).

Concerned primarily with the intersections of space, place, power, and identity, Critical Geography points to the ways in which the material, discursive, and affective work upon the bodies in particular spaces (Soja 1989; Massey and Jess 1995; Soja 1996; Harvey 2001; Allen 2003; see also Helfenbein, 2011b). This sociomaterial approach resonates with contemporary posthuman considerations that reject ontological distinctions between the human and the material. Rather, Hultin (2019) argues that the term sociomaterial itself suggests that by being

> grounded in a relational or becoming ontology (e.g. agential realism) …
> [researchers] aim to move away from a view of materiality as something
> distinct, bounded, and separate from human agency and intentionality, to
> an understanding of it as entangled with and thus, deeply co-constitutive
> of, agentic action and organizational realities.
>
> (p. 91)

From this perspective, analyses of the intersections and conjunctures of space, place, power, and identity work at once on and with/in fields of power, as well as on/in the body and its understanding of itself. As a result, place becomes a central concept as geographers—who have long insisted on careful distinctions between the concepts of space and place—turn to a focus on interrelationships. This turn to place requires a scalar approach, in that the entanglement called place includes layers as granular as the body and as broad as the world itself.

For geographers, "place" refers to a subjective understanding of a particular, localized setting: places are spaces filled with meaning for those that spend time there in particular and localized ways. Put another way, space, when constituted through discursive, interpretive, lived, affective, and imagined practices, becomes what geographers understand as place (de Certeau 1984; Soja 1996) (while imaginary geographies of place are possible, as impressions and signification can be applied to spaces one hasn't physically visited, geographers primarily focus on material spaces and our interactions with them). Place, then, has significance in complex, temporal ways that cannot be fully distinguished from the spatial. This is not to say, however, that places are in any way pristine, apolitical, or transcendent of the impact of social forces; indeed, places are particularities entangled in a myriad of relations (see Nespor 1997). Cultural, economic, and social forces work on both the inhabitants of a place and work to form the place itself. As Fataar (2019) notes, "Place is created by people while engaged in complex networks of social interactions and mental conceptualizations inside of physical spaces" (p. 26). For feminist geographers—most notably Dorren Massey—"place is a locus of complex intersections and outcomes of power geometries that operate across many spatial scales, from the body to the global" (Hubbard, Kitchin, & Valentine 2004, p. 304). This understanding of place implies that it can only be seen as possible in the multiple and fluid interactions that constitute it.

Much like the opening aperture of a camera lens, we shift focus now from the localized place to a broader globalized space. Much contemporary work in critical geography responds specifically to the complex and rapidly changing relationships of power, space, and place in late capitalism and the dynamics of global, economic, and cultural networks (Soja 1989; Massey and Jess 1995; Soja 1996; Breitbart 1998; Harvey 2001, 2005; Allen 2003). Globalization is itself a spatial term—although one used in increasingly multiple and confusing ways—and is entangled in all the complexities and changing forms of economy, sovereignty, hybridity, and culture. But space, like place, cannot be seen as a neutral tableau on which these struggles play out. Foucault (1980) reminds us that "space was treated as the dead, the fixed, the undialectical, the immobile. Time on the contrary was richness, fecundity, and life, dialectic" (p. 70). Furthermore, Soja builds on these ideas and suggests that ideology and the political cannot be teased apart from space as,

> ...it has always been political and strategic. If space has an air of neutrality and indifference with regard to its contents and thus seems to be "purely" formal, the epitome of rational abstraction, it is precisely because it has been occupied and used, and has already been the focus of past processes whose traces are not always evident on the landscape. Space has been shaped and molded from historical and natural elements, but this has been a political process. Space is political and ideological. It is a product literally filled with ideologies.
>
> (Soja, 1980, p. 207)

How *place* relates to now-globalized *space* forms a point of departure for analysis of democratic and economic relations, as well as a ground on which identity work happens.

These larger cultural forces all involve the manifestations and machinations of power within the social realm, and they work on both people and places in multiple, fluid ways. Mapping those relations of power remains a central focus of critical geographers' work, creating an affinitive connection between the field and the complementary work of critical social theory and cultural studies (in fact, these fields share foundational writers such as Marx, Lefebvre, Foucault, and

Deleuze). Some writers argue that articulating the conditions and trajectories of power and its effects on lived society are not only academic pursuits, but also an organizing core of the moral obligation of all social scientists and geographers specifically (Soja 1989; Harvey 2001). Given this, curriculum theory too embraces an analysis that situates its questions within fields of power relations not only in terms of how, why, and where curricula are produced but also in terms of how the spatial is represented.

Geography as Curriculum

Traditional geography, and certainly K12 geography education, tends to present itself as scientific and objective. While the terms space and place have certainly been foundational to the discipline of geography and geographic education, they have largely been considered bounded and fixed and not related to each other (Edwards, 2001; Gerber & Lidstone, 1996; Lambert & Machon, 2001; Morgan, 2002). As described above, however, Critical Geography rejects the neutrality of the field along with the notion that there is a singular epistemological vantage point from which the world can be described objectively (Gregory, 1978; Harvey, 1973; Massey, 1994; Rose, 1997; Said, 1978; Willinsky, 1998). It suggests instead that geography, as any other body of knowledge, is humanly constructed, and that all forms of geographic knowledge either reproduce or challenge particular knowledge, identities, and the power relations that go along with them (see Thornton, 2003). Any interpretation of the spatial carries with it assumptions, values, and perspectives about what the world is and possibly could be (see also Battimer, 1993; Davies & Gilmartin, 2002; Slater, 2001). Geography is therefore inherently a political as well as pedagogical enterprise.

The kinds of questions spatial researchers ask should thus also be political and pedagogical in nature. Some examples might include:

> What world does geography education make possible and intelligible, to whom, how, to what ends and with what consequences? How does it position those it engages to inter/act (or abstain from it) in the world, at what scales, with what purposes? Who, in current societal arrangements, has the power to "name" the world and thus determine it meaning? What power arrangements underlie the discourses made available in geography education? Who gets privileged by them, who does not?
>
> (Helfenbein, 2015, p. 402)

The new understandings of space, place, and their interaction outlined above provide significant and generative openings for educational researchers, as they help us get beyond thinking of these as "something physical and external to the social context and to social action … A context for society—its container—rather than a structure created by society" (Soja, 1980, p. 210).

Critical geographers (e.g., Gregory, 1994; Harvey, 1996; Lefebvre, 1991; Massey, 1994; Soja, 1996) have challenged the fixity of these terms, suggesting that they are socially constructed and reframing them as sets of relations that operate dialectically in the ongoing construction of subjects, who attempting to negotiate and make meaning in/through them. As such, spaces and places express ideologies, affective forces, and power relations, and are ontological processes filled with living politics that shape who we are as subjects. Considered as coming into being through the intersection of "social practices, and structures, norms and values, power and inequality, difference and distinction" (Gieryn, 2000, p. 468), space and place become "the focus of critical social analysis" (Gruenewald, 2003, p. 628). Such understandings open up potentialities for re-examining how space and place are engaged in education projects, what current manifestations promote and inhibit, as well as how these might be engaged otherwise:

> That is, what are the understandings underlying current uses of space/place and what kind of understanding do they help produce and/or mitigate among students, parents, teachers, and the community? To what degree, and how, do they allow students to think, imagine, and be in the world as they negotiate a "sense of place"? How are schools educative spaces acting on and with those that inhabit them? How are larger spatial forces such as globalized economic shifts affecting the lived experiences of schools and such theme of social education such as citizenship and democracy?
>
> (Helfenbein & Buendia, 2017, p. 29)

Employing critical understandings about space and place, however, goes beyond exploration of the terms themselves; it also provides openings to explore the implications of these considerations in social education research writ large. To understand the geographies we encounter, we need to understand the social, affective, and political processes producing them as well as their effects and the ways in which they too are produced.

Curriculum as Spatial Text

Returning to the questions that began this chapter, we turn to what it might mean to take space seriously in educational inquiry and curriculum theorizing. Curriculum as geography can be most clearly seen in the ways in which subjects find themselves mapped, bordered, defined, or even erased; but school subjects too and our conceptions of them have also been defined largely by the disciplines and date back from the turn of the century, even though this has been periodically questioned and increasingly politicized (see Kliebard 2004).

The curriculum, then maps onto school grounds, classroom design, the architectures of schools themselves, and into the lived, felt experiences of students and teachers. Interdisciplinary work, while valued in schools of education and theoretical exploration, still seems akin to a border-crossing in much of social theory. As "curriculum mapping" has become a project for aligning objectives, standards, and assessments, curriculum theorists following the lead of critical geography would rightly begin with the important caution that *maps are dangerous*. Maps define the limits to possibilities in sociomaterial situations and, therefore, the task of "curriculum mapping" must, in some way, do the same. Curriculum scholars so informed would also return to foundational commitments by interrogating how relations of power and privilege affect the creation and use of such maps.

Beyond curriculum mapping, spatial analysis is increasingly present in contemporary critical research and scholars in education are following suit. Some prominent scholars apply a spatial analysis to educative inquiry without explicitly claiming the discipline of geography: Paulo Freire's (1970) discussion of a "politics of location"; classroom geographies (Johnson, 1982; McKinney, 2000); Nespor's (1997) *Tangled Up in School*; and cultural studies approaches to education (Dimitriadis & Carlson, 2003; Hytten 1999; Giroux, 2000). There are various ethnographies about specific school spaces and the lives of students, such as Eckert (1989), McLaren's *Life in Schools* (2003/1994), Valenzuela (1999), Yon (2000), and Pope (2001), to name only a few. Of course, there are books that address geography as a subject, as in elementary education (i.e., Sobel, 1998), or secondary social studies education (i.e., Kincheloe 2001; Segal & Helfenbein 2008; Schmidt & Kenreich, 2015). Certainly, there are other books that have taken on the notion of place, such as Pinar and Kincheloe's *Curriculum as Social Psychoanalysis: The Significance of Place* (1991), and McLaren's *Life in Schools* (1994). David Hutchison's *A Natural History of Place in Education* (2004) and David Greenwood's (2003; formerly Gruenwald) influential *Educational Researcher* article "The Best of Both Worlds: A Critical Pedagogy of Place" provides significant inquiry into the use of place as a theoretical concept applied to schools. While critical geographers are not necessarily used in these works and they make no mention of the framework proper, some of the concerns inherent to critical geography are taken up by these various scholars (e.g., identity and power in relation to conceptions of place). However, the language and authors of critical geography are evoked in other work, such as Hongyu Wang's (2004) *The Call from the Stranger on a Journey Home: Curriculum in a Third Space*. Furthermore, other movements in educational research that engage analysis of space and/or place, particularly in recent publications and presentations, demonstrate the timeliness of this book's exploration.

In terms of this more contemporary work, critical scholars have taken up inquiry around school spaces and their relation to students, parents, and educators, notably around issues of LGBTQ youth and students of color. Schmidt (2015) offers that "if injustice is written into space, then a curricular challenge is how to understand inequity through space and produce responses that reorganize space" (p. 254). Buendía, Ares, Juarez & Peercy's (2004) important article on school reform states that,

> race- and class-based topographies of east and west, as is the case in this reform, the durability of these constructs thwarts change. These constructs, as assemblages of local and national discourses around race, class, and schooling, both organize and are organized by material relations that are integrated into school practice, epistemologies, and technologies (e.g., funding, curriculum).
>
> (p. 835)

Mapping students' conceptions of space and place comprises not just theory but method in Wozolek's (2018) critical ethnographic inquiry into the experiences of students of color. Other examples of contemporary work include: Schmidt's (2011) analysis of place-making and students' spatial understanding outside school; an exploration of Latina/o students in ethnic studies courses and the spatial implications of pedagogy as the role of "academic space" (Marrun, 2018); Nakagawa & Payne's (2016) landscape ethnography of an environmental program and learners' understandings of those spaces; geospatial understandings around activism and educational issues (Nguyen, Cohen, & Huff, 2017); Blockett's (2017) inquiry on the possibilities of "black queer space" in higher education; Gershon's (2017) inquiry on sound and identity in racialized spaces and exploration into how "sounds create spaces that can further limit or supersede physical boundaries…denote historical time and value…and serve as markers between spaces, delineating one space or idea from another" (2018, p.15); and Charteris, Smardon, Foulkes, & Bewley's (2016) work on new materialist assemblages as biographical, embodied spaces.

Similarly, the production of queer spaces and the ways in which they are policed points to an analysis of queer identity formation that includes how spaces can be understood as queer or straight, and how attendant behaviors come to be regulated within those spaces. Scholars of LGBTQ experiences thus highlight the role of space in inquiry into marginalization and resistance. Tierney and Ward (2017) state that "Critical geography provides a lens to understand the movements and daily lives of LGBT homeless youth" (p. 504). The role of New Orleans' performative spaces foregrounds Love's (2017) exploration of the spatial aspects of gender and sexual identity as a part of her proposal for a "ratchet lens" in qualitative studies of black queer youth. Finally, Mayo (2017) offers that LGBTQ scholars as a whole point to how "location can help shape understandings of subjectivities that are emergent within social networks and institutions" (p. 535).

Place also plays a foundational role in Indigenous methodologies and ways of knowing. Indigenous scholars working in educational theorizing point to the ontological implications of a priori relations between subject and place (Marker, 2018, Grande & McCarty, 2018; Lipe & Lipe, 2016; Friedel, 2014), but also expand their critique to the broader dynamic of settler colonialism (Grande & McCarty, 2018; Francis & Munson, 2016; Nxumalo, 2016). Combining place and storytelling, Somerville (2014) highlights "the potential of place as a conceptual framework for connecting the local and global, the real and symbolic, the individual and the collective, and our inner sense of ourselves with the external world" (p. 80). Inverting traditional binaries in research, this insistence on the entanglements of body and place offers an attempt to put Western and indigenous ways of knowing into conversation with respect to educational theory. Again, while not necessarily using the specific terms of Critical Geography or even spatial theory, these scholars point to indigenous processes of meaning-making and the onto-epistemological implications of material spaces in ways that resonate with this field. Not only does this work challenge the white, Western dominance of social theory, it also suggests that it is precisely this dominance that obscures potential new understandings of curriculum. Clearly, work on how these considerations play out in schools and curriculum represents an important addition to educational and curriculum theorizing.

Global–Local Curriculum

Pulling out in focus from particular studies to broader questions of the spatiality of the sociomaterial, we attend to issues of space, scale, and curriculum. As many have noted, the foundational question of curriculum remains—although certainly not untroubled: "what knowledge is of most worth?" (Spencer 1859; Pinar 2004). As we know that schools cannot teach *everything*, the process of creating curriculum is, by definition, exclusionary. This simple fact pushes curriculum considerations into the ethical, as decisions about what is included and what is not must be made. One way to frame this struggle could be to balance the local and the global. Seemingly contradictory, it can be useful to think here in scalar terms, emphasizing the changing scales of analysis that put these forces in relation. Questions of curriculum reform often attend to concerns about the global economy and the workforce of the future. Public rhetoric around schools revolves around the new conditions of an increasingly globalized economy and deep-seated fears that schools may be "behind the curve." At the same time, greater attention to teaching "urban kids," or, more specifically, black and Hispanic students, points toward localized spaces and the particularities of certain populations with racialized histories and geographies. Culturally relevant pedagogy, anti-racist education, and a resurgence of vocational education, online education, charter schools, and privatization are all offered as potential answers. Curriculum reform with one eye on the global workplace and the other on particular needs of local communities presents challenges and complexity. These challenges are better addressed with curriculum theorizing and educational policy work that takes up the "yes, and" offered by a scalar approach than with the "either, or" of a bifurcated view.

Critical geography and its scalar approach to analysis—or, as I have called it, the geography of the "yes, and"—insists on attention to both the global and the local, not only in the sense of assessing the needs of the future workers but also in creating critical understanding of the present conditions that students, teachers, and parents find themselves in. The localized context of access to education, job opportunities, obstacles to academic achievement, and even school funding are in no way separate from the responses to global economic forces by multiple levels of government and business interests. Urban settings provide the most condensed site for analyses of these processes, and urban education reform exhibits all the characteristics of changing spatial ordering and prioritization, as well as demonstrating the impact of new demographic and socio-economic shifts. In response, much of critical geography has turned to analysis of how the conditions of late capitalism and globalized interconnection impact the changing relationships between space and place (Soja 1989; Massey & Jess 1995; Soja 1996; Breitbart 1998; Harvey 2001; Allen 2003). At the same time, education scholars have begun to question not only "the racial segregation of space but also to ask questions about the knowledge that is possible within particular spaces, as well as the effect this knowledge has on these spaces" (Buendía & Ares 2006, p. 836). This relational understanding of spaces extends into onto-epistemological territory, as the sociomaterial holds deep implications for knowing/being/doing. Analyses of economic relations, political economy, democratic reform, citizenship, and sovereignty all become points of departure for mapping relations of power as part of understanding place related to an increasingly globalized space.

Concluding Thoughts and the Journey Ahead

The role of research in educational theorizing and curriculum studies should be greater than simply providing information on what works in the classroom. Claiming a role in challenging disciplinary and pedagogical assumptions, identifying underpinning values and biases, and asking critical questions about purposes (Roberts, 2000, p. 290) allows for a more critical, robust scholarship on this place called school. By incorporating critical geography understandings in these analyses, we can help confront disciplinary "assumptions and biases, to contextualize issues and situate them within social horizons, to view landscapes as the outcome of actors enabled and constrained by their historical environment—that is, to engage them with theory" (Warf, 1997, p. 85). This move away from research that adheres to disciplinary understandings to one that critically examines them and pays attention to the ways in which spaces and places—and the various understanding that go along with them—"are made, imagined, contested, and enforced" (Gupta & Ferguson, 1992, p. 18) embodies the essence of the critical, spatial turn in geography.

Whether we consider the impact of critical geography on educational research and theorizing or take up a critique of the ways in which the spatial has been represented in the formal curriculum, reconsidering the entanglement of space, place, power, and identity offers new possibilities for insight into the lived experience of school and other educative spaces. To privilege a sociomaterial approach that not only includes the discursive, affective, and material creates a critical geography that puts these forces in relation, always already entangled and enables a critique that aligns with new developments in affect theory, new materialisms, and the posthuman. The insistence on the material within this work precedes some of the contemporary theorizing with which I hope to connect and comes from this geographer's commitment to place and feminist geography's privileging of the body as a locus of analysis. In many ways, what I have presented in this chapter is an intellectual history of the specific ideas of critical geography and how they might overlap and thread through other advances in attempts at better understanding the world. Not meant to be a complete list, the hope is that I have laid enough of a foundation in order to begin this intellectual geography so that the reader might see where it has taken me since the first steps on this path; in addition, the hope lies in the promise that readers might see where they too might go, what avenues might open up, what spaces of possibilities are yet to be uncovered in educational inquiry and curriculum theorizing.

Let's go.

Notes

1 I am indebted to Walter Gershon for many things represented in this volume but his conception of being/knowing/doing as the necessarily entangled product of education is noted here; see Gershon 2017.
2 For Barad /(2007), the term intra-action (as opposed to interaction) "signifies the mutual constitution of entangled agencies" (p.33) and denotes agency as dynamism and the impossibility of objectivity.

2

SPACE, PLACE, AND POWER

Driving into town from the University of North Carolina—Chapel Hill to Raleigh, I follow a highway that shows the dramatic consequences of urban sprawl and considerable development since I was a kid. The interstate traverses the state from East to West following historical routes of train and track. The city that developed on this route soon expanded beyond a stop on a long interstate to include a loop around the city's core which allowed for traffic to bypass the growing urban area. What was once a scenic wooded and farmed route now stalls with traffic and unending construction, blurring the lines between communities that were once distinct and seemed far away. As a turn in the highway projects cars into the city of Raleigh avoiding the multi-laned loop, neighborhoods rather suddenly line the street in intimate ways; we are now in the city proper. The houses that border the busy street reflect an aesthetic of days gone by; spacious and brick, the homes sit on wooded lots with mature oak and pine shading both the houses and the street. This is an old, moneyed neighborhood. This is the neighborhood that surrounds William W. Holden High School.

Turning off of the main thoroughfare that brings cars and trucks straight into downtown onto a perpendicular street—named for the all-girls college, started in 1842, two blocks to the south—leads to the impressive high school building on the corner of an intersection. The rear of the building—a recent addition—stands as a modern, brick square enclosing a gated courtyard overlooking the bus parking lot and limited student parking spots. Closer to the intersection, the older portion of the school—at the time, under reconstruction—rises to unusual heights with a large clock tower in the center. Made of quarried stone, the building has the appearance of a fortified building laid out on a wide lawn. Wide steps spread out before me at the front of the building. These are the steps that governors have been inaugurated on and the students of downtown Raleigh have tread for decades. That is to say, 'certain' students of Raleigh have trod those steps and benefited from these histories and traditions.

Across the street from the school lies an unassuming building, presumably (by the looks of it) built in the seventies as some form of office complex. It is small and functional, steel and glass, striking a notable contrast to the decorative, elaborate stonework of the school across the street. Three stories with much smaller steps facing the street, the building holds Holden's profile in prime view. The bottom two floors of this structure house the William Edenton's Learning Lab (WELL) and through its doors pass mainly students of Holden High School. On the school side of the street is a busy city bus stop offering students transportation deeper into the heart of downtown. On the WELL side, the return route, going out to the suburbs, is marked by a different type of rider waiting for the bus—not students of Holden, but workers off to take their place in the more plentiful retail jobs of strip malls and fast food that characterize urban sprawl. The inner-city students who ride the Capital Area Transit Bus (CAT) or "the city-kitty," as the kids refer to it, exit the bus two doors down from the WELL in the early morning before first period and climb back aboard at various times after Holden's last bell, returning to very different "downtown" neighborhoods than the one surrounding the high school.

The street that passes in front of Holden leads to an outdoor shopping mall to the north and the revitalized downtown district to the south. The shopping mall—once the radical vision and later pride of the city developers—holds expensive specialty shops, restaurants, a branch of the public library, a large grocery store that reflects the new multi-use design that includes amenities such as coffee bar and food court type facilities. It sits close to a major university, and a variety of patrons come and go in the mall. To the south on this busy street lies a taqueria (notably new), two convenience stores, and a McDonalds fast food restaurant. Past these establishments are a Starbucks coffee and the beginnings of a thriving restaurant and bar area. Construction seems to be constant with condominiums being built and old buildings in varying states of remodeling.

To continue further into downtown Raleigh, one sees the site of local and state government, a banking and finance center, and the continued stirrings of a downtown revitalization effort. Very little housing remains in these areas besides the expensive condominiums being erected either in bulldozed corners of the old downtown or in refurbished buildings. An expanding wealthy, historical district lies to the east with the clear process of gentrification at work on the often dilapidated homes of the neighborhood. On every visit to the area, the line between run-down houses with several tenants and refitted Victorian homes seems to shift toward the latter. Despite the development, the poverty of the adjacent neighborhoods is tangible. Two homeless shelters and several substance abuse centers sit in the along this tenuous border. Farther to the south of the center of downtown lies the public housing project of Travis Hills—the other, closer to the historical district was recently bulldozed to build more condominiums.

The lines between the different people of downtown Raleigh were much clearer in the days of segregation. Not only before the efforts to rebuild downtown, but in the days before downtown Raleigh lost its place as focal point for the burgeoning city, the simple grid system of the streets held important marker and meaning to its inhabitants. Hargett Street, a mere three blocks from Holden High School, was a bustling economic center for the black community of Raleigh. Segregation in full effect by the 1920's, the street served the black neighborhoods that occupied the south and east portions of the city. A City Market, situated between the black community of Hargett and the government and finance area that surrounded the capital, served as a space of limited and occasional integration. People of both races, wealthy and poor, would come into the market to buy meat, vegetables and flowers until the 1950's brought the rise of suburbs and the spread of Raleigh outside the highway loop.

As the city of Raleigh went through these changes, the effects were felt at Holden High School. To wind our way back from the once thriving Hargett area, we travel east past the City Market, now a gentrified multi-use area with expensive, trendy stores, an interactive museum with IMAX Theater, and offices, bars and restaurants; this is the New South[1]. Soon however we cross into a less developed area—the edge of gentrification—marked by the overtaxed homeless shelter and a small row of Habitat for Humanity houses. To turn south and begin our loop around we see more and more urban deterioration. Houses that once were simple but coveted residences now slump in disrepair and the neighborhood always seems to have small groups of men loitering on porches and corners. Crossing back to the west, south of Hargett Street, we see more of the same rows of houses in disrepair until we come to the recently expanded Memorial Auditorium and seventies era Civic Center. At this point, we quickly find ourselves in the scattered projects of renewal and new construction. Empty storefronts contrast with ambitious entrepreneurs hoping to be on the cusp of the economic turnaround. The capital and government buildings still hum with activity during the workday but quickly become a part of the eerie, empty silence in most parts of the area by night. But to move north and east, just to the edge of what has historically been called downtown Raleigh, we return to the imposing campus of William W. Holden High School and, across the street, its oddly shaped counterpart, the WELL.

Place-Making at the WELL

The William Edenton Learning Lab (hereafter referred to as the WELL), created in 1996 as a function of the William Edenton Foundation in Raleigh, North Carolina, provides an after-school computer lab for the students of Holden High School and the Wake County Public Schools[2]. Designed to provide access to information technology and tutorial resources, the WELL hoped to become a prototype for community centers that bridge the gap between school and society through the use of technology. The mission of the non-profit program revolved around providing a place where students can both supplement their academic work and skills in using information technology and provide opportunities for remedial skill development. Located adjacent to William W. Holden High School, the WELL offered a staffed computer lab and after-school tutorial services from 3–10 pm every Sunday through Thursday and from 3–7 pm on Fridays. Room for studying and access to internet equipped computers and tutors from the Holden National Honor Society comprise the services offered to all students. During my time there, a number of students frequently spent their after-school hours at the WELL and, as projects at Holden came and went, the attendance fluctuated accordingly.

This chapter chronicles the beginning of this journey toward applying Critical Geography to educational research and curriculum theorizing as it quickly became clear that place-making and identity work were central to what was going on at the WELL. My dissertation project at UNC-Chapel Hill inquired about the students who embraced the WELL as a supplement to their high school experience, what, in their minds, the WELL offered them and their peers—what made this space different from the spaces of school. In pursuit of those goals, beginning to think in a critical geography framework enabled me to interrogate how the students made place within the intersections of space, power, and identity. Students indeed made meaning at the WELL, constructing an alternative community—revolving around but not solely about technology— to the social structure in which they usually saw themselves. Their constructions were in important ways spatial, representing a set of divides: in/out, home/ school, school/not-school, and WELL community/urban community. The lessons learned from the stories of these students speak to broader issues related to youth and youth culture that connect to their navigation of social networks, urban education, and educative spaces, and the construction and re-constructions of student identity.

The accounts of students who spent time at the WELL revolved around notions of place. Place, distinguished from space in that it is *made* within the context of broader formations (i.e., topography, society, culture, economics, and affect[3]), describes a set of relations. Often in opposition to those broader spatial formations, place is an idea. The alternative community constructed by the students at the WELL began with a crossing of the street that forms a border between school and something else. This border crossing was significant not only in its immediate spatial distinctions, but also metaphorically in the sense of identity that students took up. Students spoke of themselves as uniquely not "over there," referring to the spaces that make up the school grounds. For these reasons, my analysis takes up the work of critical geography and cultural studies to explore notions of space and place and their connections to identity.

Perhaps strangely, youth cultures and scholarly attention to them has held something of a marginal place in educational scholarship. Often tangled up in notions of deviance, delinquency, consumerism, and violence, *youth* as a category continues to hold something of a liminal position, "ambiguously wedged between childhood and adulthood" (Valentine, Skelton, & Chambers, 1998, p. 4). This category of youth shifts and adapts in response to the social, cultural, and economic shifts—material, discursive, and affective—taking place all around it. Fine and Weiss (1998) note how working-class youth often find themselves characterized and politically and culturally employed by forces in search of explanatory narratives and scapegoats.

> [T]hey are displayed and dissected in the media as the cause of national problems. They are depicted as the *reason* for the rise in urban crime, as

embodying the *necessity* for welfare reform, and of sitting at the *heart* of moral decay.

(p. 1, *author's emphasis*)

Referring to the "dilemma of the postmodern childhood," Steinberg and Kincheloe (1997) suggest the increasing importance of studying youth culture in order to understand late capitalism (see also Grossberg, 2005; Helfenbein 2006b). The WELL provided an opportunity to learn about particular aspects of youth culture tied to particular spatial dynamics and processes of making place under conditions not of their own making.

For some time, geographies of youth culture have reinforced the notion that public space continues to be defined as adult space. Youth then resist and negotiate in the struggle to create youth places out of adult spaces. These ways in which youth strive for a sense of place, identity, and expression are varied and vary in terms of their success and sustainability (Breitbart, 1998). Although the WELL was intended for academic work—notably with no set curriculum in the formal sense (see Helfenbein 2006a)—it allowed students to police themselves for the most part. This too created the conditions for a liminal character: neither school nor home, public nor private, but rather a conglomeration of both. It was a place in which the students themselves played a significant role in fashioning its meaning. It is in this sense that critical geography can help us better understand this particular place and the students that spent time there.

Crossing the Street

The WELL, as all places, exists situated within a larger historical, contextual space. This context includes the tangible aspects of urban geographies, the physical possibilities for access, the historical meanings of spaces and places, and the constructed social meanings of spatial relationships. The narrative drive through Raleigh to the WELL and its surroundings that begins this chapter is meant to introduce the complexities of a place with the hope of learning something about how young people navigate and negotiate those spaces to create place. The students in this study come from various places on this narrative map of the city of Raleigh. The "downtown people"—a phrase that becomes important in the stories told by participants—live in the neighborhoods directly surrounding Holden and sharing its zip code. Less than 2% of students who have attended the WELL (outside of the mandatory freshman technology orientation) and none of the students in this study live in these neighborhoods. The "bus-pass kids," who only pass through the WELL and similarly only pass through this story, live in the downtown areas marked by large minority populations and low socioeconomic level, including the public housing project of Travis Hills. How gentrification of the urban center will affect these students remains to be seen and could open further critical geography inquiry about those places. Brian, Emily, and Jennie

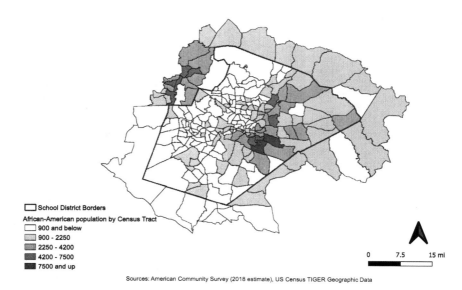

MAP 1 Racial Demographics of Wake County Public Schools: Raleigh, NC and Surroundings.

are "WELL Kids" that participated in this study that all live in these downtown spaces and are all, notably, black. The other students—white, black, Latino, and Asian—live outside the multi-laned highway that encircles the urban core of Raleigh, some as far away as small towns over an hour to the north only recently seen as a suburb of the city.

The space of Holden High School is formed in relation to other schools in the district and in students' prior experiences. At the time, Holden had been recently designated as a magnet school in the county which meant that the student population now came from areas throughout the growing urban/suburban complex. A school that once consisted of the sons and daughters of the wealthy elite expanded its population as a result of desegregation, school redistricting, and a move to magnet status. The WELL, started through the philanthropic efforts of a successful attorney, states the "digital divide" of access to information technology between white and black and rich and poor, as its reason for existence. The main purpose of the facility was to provide computer access and computer training to the students who do not have either the technology or the skills. The school came to depend on the WELL to provide a space for the students to come and use the technology for school assignments and research.

In 1997, I made the drive to Holden High School described in the preceding opening to this chapter. I was returning to the city of my adolescence to apply for a teaching position. While further work in graduate school tempted me, the interview at Holden—the "flagship" of the state's schools as it was referred to—proved to be more than I could turn down. The assistant principal who interviewed and ultimately recommended me for hiring stopped the formalities short when I asked about the role of technology at Holden. At this point, she immediately took me up to the media center to speak with the parent volunteer who headed up the efforts to "bring Holden into the Information Age." I had apparently asked a good question. The WELL had been mentioned that day as a symbol of their efforts to integrate technology into the everyday curriculum of the school and soon after my hiring I was involved in the efforts to do so. Before school even started that year, I crossed the street to the WELL.

Coming into Place

Question: Why do these kids come to the WELL?

Answer: … they get what they need

Access to information technology, being the justification for the existence of WELL in the late 90s, was both the original attraction for students and a continuing form of cultural capital for the students who regularly spent time there. Notably at this time, knowledge and skills related to information technology was both sought after and compiled for social advantage. It quickly became clear that the WELL held a particular place at the intersection of race, class, gender, and the importance of this emerging knowledge. The multiple stories told by the participants show the complexities of attempting to understand any social space, or to understand the multiple identities that students inhabit in the course of their everyday lives. Central themes in the stories of students who regularly attended the WELL were safety, mobility, social hierarchy, and navigating the realities of urban communities. While information technology was an incentive for participation, what compelled students to be "a WELL kid" was much more of a response to exclusionary realities of both a highly structured school and the dangers of homelife, both perceived and real.

The WELL resonated with these discourses of safety, social hierarchy, and urban realities, echoing and competing for attention. By sifting through, filtering, centering and decentering, and mapping those multiple discourses—in other words, trying to make sense of them—the fundamental purpose of my study emerged. The complexity, multiplicity, and fluidity of this place became clear—it moved. I asked: How did these students come to be in this place? How do they *make* place? In what ways do they make sense of it and how are those senses formed? What is the broader context of these interactions and how could I learn about the relationships involved in educative space from these student stories? Place as a concept became important for me early on in my observations. It seemed that the particularities of this place were different—different

from the school across the street, different from the parking lot or the convenience store where other kids hung out, and different from other computer
labs I had observed. This place was different, and different in the sense that it
was defined not only by borders and divides but also in the negotiation of and
resistance to those demarcations. How the students set up and transgressed those
borders *became* the study.

As I spent more time with these students it became clear to me that a story
of the WELL was about how young people navigate the spaces imposed on them
and begin to make *places*. Places are spaces imbued with meaning. How the students and staff worked at making a place out of the William Edenton Learning
Lab reveals not only things about these particular young people and the structures
that work on them, but also speaks of the relationships between youth and their
peers, youth and school, youth and home, and youth and community. The place
made at the WELL serves not only as an entangled intersection of these varied
and scalar forces, but it is also a place of opposition or perhaps, more accurately,
negotiation. Moving toward a critical geography frame proved useful as a way to
think about these students in that process of negotiation.

As a brief example, I turn to an afternoon early in the semester that I spent
at the front desk of the WELL, watching the comings and goings of students,
the interactions of staff, and coming to a sense of how this place feels. It was
yearbook day and much like my memories of classroom teaching, the exchange
and careful study of the annuals held prominent position in the students' attention. The first incident of note occurred when it was pointed out—with mock
surprise—that the wrong photo had been included for the page dedicated to the
WELL. Instead of the posed staff photo, the image depicted a camping trip that
was attended by both students and staff. Two reactions quickly swirled around
the desk: the first being a resignation that of course the yearbook staff got it
wrong because those students have nothing to do with the WELL, and the
second being a mild form of terror—as if the students in the picture had, in a
way, been outed. These two reactions reflect the sense of distance, an opposition to the social hierarchy of the high school that pervades this study. A position on the yearbook staff is a coveted honor among the elite of Holden for
both college application value and its reputation as a relatively easy course. The
instructor in charge hand selects the group based on Grade Point Average and
teacher recommendations. The reaction by these students shows how the WELL
is used by students and not taken up as an identity claim. When asked if friends
at school knew that a student daily attended the WELL, one student's response
was emphatic "No, thank God!"

Later that afternoon, I noticed the spine of the yearbook. It was embossed
with the name of the school, the city, and the zip code—no street address. I wondered aloud about why they would print the zip code. I didn't remember that
being the case when I taught at this school—this was later confirmed by looking

at a 2000 copy—and then began to think of the particular geography of this particular school. The neighborhood around the school is a historic one filled with large homes, prominent churches, and the local country club. The people that lived in this neighborhood were the people that shared this zip code—it became very clear that these were not the students who attended the WELL. So, I began to think of the use of this zip code in something of the way that I understand Manhattanites use the area code 212 or community activists in Baltimore use the zip code 21217—to signify their difference, an identity claim. To think in this way resembles traditional notions of place and identity and the resultant conflation that critical geography troubles.

This is how, I suggest, the students engage in an economy of identities. The school as place is still present in the WELL—they are, after all, doing homework, working on projects, and, in their own words, "getting what they need." But the students *use*—and interestingly do not *take up*—the WELL in order to navigate the larger structures of school, community, and youth itself. As I construct a map of this place, I argue that data gathered in conversations like these with students are examples of how they have made place—in multiple ways—in opposition to the place of the school across the street, while still exhibiting many of the characteristics evident within the attendant social relations.

As critical geography points out, the position of the cartographer has much to do with the nature of the map. It is therefore important to note my own relationships with the WELL and Holden High School early in the introduction of this inquiry. While the connections with the WELL during my graduate study appeared through opportune coincidence (the director of the WELL made a presentation to interested students and faculty in the hopes of its potential as a research site and I happened to be recruited by the Dean of the School of Education), my interest in the lab and its students was rekindled as I thought back on my 3 years as a social studies teacher at Holden. Even then I remember feeling that "something" was going on across the street at the WELL that was at least interesting in that students chose to spend time there after school. At that point, looking at the lab from the vantage point within the boundaries of the school, my understanding of what this place meant to students and what exactly went on there remained a mystery. We, the teachers of Holden, knew that supposedly positive things occurred there as the school touted its existence in the efforts of self-promotion but had no real sense of which students spent time there, how they spent that time, or how the efforts related to the students' experiences at Holden High School. So then, this chapter resonates with my own stories of the school at which I taught and those of the students that I came to know both in my history as a teacher there and later as a researcher at the lab. Brought together in the following section, the stories presented here are *my own* map of the relations of these students and the terrain of school, WELL, home, and world.

Stories from the WELL

> Through stories about places, they become inhabitable. Living is narrativ-
> izing. Stirring up or restoring this narrativizing is thus also among the tasks
> of renovation. One must awaken the stories that sleep in the streets...
> Festivals, contests, the development of 'speaking places' in neighborhoods
> or buildings would return to narratives the soil from which they grow.
> (De Certeau, Mayol, & Tomasik, 1998, pp. 142–143)

The *place*ness of the WELL is defined by the multiplicity of stories that students
tell about themselves, the WELL, and why young people come there. In the
construction of this particular map of the WELL—particular in that another
cartographer would undoubtedly build it differently—certain types of stories
help organize a characterization of this place. As John Pickles (2004) reminds us,
geography is the story of a finger and an eye. The finger draws the viewer's eye,
or attention, to an object or place amongst a larger, fluid field. The types of stories presented here, marked by individual stories from the students interviewed,
comprise the objects to which my mapmaker's finger points.

A Researcher's Story

Just as I had on my first day as a teacher several years earlier, in 2003 I crossed
the street again. Parking—out of habit, I think—in the teacher's parking lot,
I had come to do some preliminary observations of the WELL. As I got out of
my car, I looked up at the bell tower and stone masonry of the school building
and thought about the 3 years I had spent there as a social studies teacher; those
long days seemed like a long time ago and yet, the gravel beneath my feet and
the sounds of students milling about after school still felt familiar. Walking to the
front door of the WELL, I looked both ways on the often busy street seeing the
flank of the school complex meandering to the north and the city skyline rising
to the south. Turning away from the school complex and the city at large and
entering the large glass doors of the building, I felt as though I had entered a
doctor's office or trendy business. The reception area with countertop and desk/
computer space behind begs the question, "can I help you?" But in this case, no
one made such a query. The building appeared empty, oddly quiet in the way
school classrooms are on teacher workdays or the weekend. Yet, the school day
continued across the street. In another 15 minutes the bell would sound and this
place would rapidly fill up with students. Taking a seat at the front desk felt a little
presumptuous but seemed to be a good vantage point for the coming activity.

After a few moments, the director of the WELL, Steve, walked by and nod-
ded, followed by a staff member, the only one who works during the day. There
seemed to be a sense that the students would soon be here. The bells of the
school cannot be heard inside the WELL, but the immediate exit by students

from several doors across the street signals the end of the school day. A few students, backpacks weighing them down, slowly made their way to the front steps of the WELL. Jack, a former student at Holden and now full-time staffer, and Steve meandered to the front steps, greeting and mingling with the first students to arrive. A combination of staff members and regulars, the group who comes immediately at the bell knows one another and speaks cordially.

The students sign in at the reception desk, lug their backpacks into the computer room or the downstairs study area, and drop their burdens like dead weight on the floor or table. Other students slowly trickle in from the sidewalk and stairs outside, clearly taking more time before entering the WELL. Conversations, often yelled across the street and parking lot, bounce back and forth amongst those who keep walking down the sidewalk, undoubtedly heading for the McDonald's or the Seven-Even [sic] convenience store, and those who veer off to enter the WELL. Meanwhile student and parent traffic flows out of the Holden parking lots, oblivious to this smaller building across the street. The school buses only occasionally pass, as the lot for them is at the opposite end of the school from the WELL. Many students as well, those with cars, leave from the back parking lots even further away than the bus lots. The after-school trajectory of most students, those who ride the bus and those who drive or carpool, notably moves away from the WELL.

Getting up to move into the lab room, I see students continually moving about the room creating an odd sense of controlled chaos. The sounds of conversations retelling the events of the school day, and the printer continually clicking off documents for waiting students fill the room with a kind of hum, an electric feel to the hour just after school is out. English, Spanish, academic, and hip-hop languages all resonate within the room. The director and his assistants roam through the lab, mostly stopping to answer a quick question rather than to direct activities. This place seems to run itself. The computer lab of the WELL is today packed with approximately 33 people; it's crowded. The comings and goings make setting a number difficult. It's busier than I will learn is usual but most seem content with their ability to access the computers or their friends.

At another moment, I attempted to assess the demographic makeup of the computer lab, counting 21 African-Americans, 5 Caucasians, 2 Hispanics, and 1 Asian. The director of the program was in and out of the lab, as were the two student assistants who circulated socializing and answering technical questions. The director made an overly obvious display of his attention to what was on the screens of the computers. The students were supposed to notice. An office with observation type windows is situated in the corner of the lab. Students directed questions there when a roving assistant was not available. Following the director's lead, my own quick scan of the computer screens noted most on the internet, some in email, and a small number in word processing programs or spreadsheets. Books and notebooks filled the spaces between the computers and book bags cluttered the walking space. Generally, I came to learn the patterns in the lives of high school students that affect this place: the intensity of exam time, the distraction of school dances, how well the girls' soccer team is doing this year, and so on.

Focusing on half the lab, two groups of students seemed actively engaged in some form of assignment. Although frequently interrupted by passersby, both groups returned to the task in front of them. Group 1 was working on a word processing document. The three female, two white and one black, all huddled around the computer screen and struggled with what appeared to be formatting an outline in Microsoft Word. The black student seemed to be in the role of writing the paper, while the two other students advised. At one point, a student jokingly commented, "You're not very computer literate, are you?" Laughs ensued by all. Continual questions and answers bounced back and forth between the girls with one student occasionally addressing her math homework spread out on her lap.

Group 2 consisted of two black students browsing through internet sites. A notebook and textbook strewn between them, the students conversed and compared the information found to a drawing of some sort of geographic formation. The male student seemed to be the most involved as evidenced by his female partner occasionally slipping over to check her open email account. Often the male student, brow furrowed, would hold up the crayon drawing to the screen, checking for comparable images. As these examples indicate, most of the help and instruction given comes from other students working in the lab. The director and assistants focus their attention on keeping the machines running and seem to pause in mid-stride to answer questions.

In the second half of the room, four students against the wall were playing some form of text-based online game. Their screens rolled vertically with text of yellow, red, and green against a black background. One student hovered behind their chairs and took notes on a legal pad. Occasional groans of distress or exultations of pleasure emanated from the group. The group, which clearly became a unified collection of interactive activity, included two whites, one Asian, and one black student. Eventually, more students entered the lab. They began milling around, seemingly nervous and impatient. Apparently, different from earlier in the observation, students now needed the computers. An assistant eventually, after making sure the new lab goers were serious about doing academic work, asked the gamers to give up their seats to the other students. Without any ado, the students complied.

A parent walked into the WELL, talking on a cell phone, obviously looking for her child. After some scanning of the room, she asked some students. One volunteered, "you looking for Jackie?" The parent was told that her daughter was at the school working on another assignment and left to find her. Cell phones rang, the printer kept printing, and the conversation kept rolling. My experiences as a teacher years past brought certain things to my eye, influenced the map I would come to make. For me, the seamless collaboration across gender and racial groups was unusual in comparison to what I know about the school across the street and the entrance of the adult served to highlight the youth-centered nature of this place. My map of this place had already been written before I drew a single line; the mapmaker is as much the map as its creator.

Stories of Change

Brian, an African-American senior, commented on how the WELL has changed since he has attended. Mobility and transit are a part of his story but, most interestingly, he offers that the changes at the WELL are a result of the influx of magnet students—like Jim. Brian, a self-described "band kid," describes a connection with many of the staff members who were also at one time in band. The after-school practice schedule of the highly respected band creates transportation issues for many of the members.

BRIAN Um, I'm a senior. I'm in band. I've been in band four years at Holden. I do a lot of community service. I got the Presidential Service Award this year…I'm just really into music. Um, pretty good in grades. I'm going to East Carolina next year.

R Why do you come to the WELL?

BRIAN Um, you come to do homework, but it's also–like a lot of other schools have–I don't know, they don't really have places to hang out. This is like a–there's not more–I know some people think of it like a hangout, but it's– You can kind of hang out here, but do your homework with friends, like not by yourself. That's why I enjoy it.

R When you come here, what, what do you mostly do?

BRIAN Um, I do homework and then I talk to friends, socializing… [pause] That's one of the reasons I like it here. Um, I don't usually have a lot of–I've had a lot of projects this year…that need to be done on a computer. I do have a computer at home, but dial-up takes forever and so it's better here.

R Are you mostly downstairs doing homework or conference room or… BRIAN: Um, usually I'm in the conference room. Either if I'm like–if I don't eat lunch or if I need to like eat something I'll be there, but I'm in the computer lab most of the time.

R Why do you think when you've eluded–you've hinted at it–what, what about other people? Why, why do they come to the WELL?

BRIAN Um, I know a lot of people come to socialize. It's gotten worse…since my freshman year. Like, I think part of the problem–part of the reason is Holden became a magnet school.

So, not all them people have the–know that this is not just like a–it's not a hangout. It's more of a social learning environment…[pause] that's when I hate coming over here. It's when I like go somewhere else or go walk in the storeroom.

But, um, I still do like it, it's just by 4:00 most of them leave and it's pretty cool and quiet. You can usually do your homework.

R It's the magnet school kids that didn't understand how the WELL is supposed to work? Is that what you're...

BRIAN Like since Holden became a magnet—well, yeah, since it became a magnet, it's been big variety. I guess Holden's more crowded. It means more people over here and, yeah.

R Freshman year it was...

BRIAN It was really nice. Sophomore year too, even though we started being a magnet sophomore year. It was still nice over here. Junior year, that's when it started to get more crowded.

For Brian, Holden's shift to a magnet school—which brings in students from all the surrounding communities—created an influx of youth who did not understand the rules of behavior expected at the WELL. Brian admits the social aspects of spending time at the WELL, but implies that this is always mixed with the ability to finish homework, work collaboratively, or get help. The magnet school kids, in his view, have dropped the academic piece to the detriment of the whole community. He also rightly recognizes the increased student population across the street and suggests that some of the issues at the WELL are simply the result of new students and higher numbers.

The students who attended the WELL lived a highly mobile life. Everyone knows the difficulty of moving when a person is young—new friends, new neighborhood, and, most frightening of all, new school. Many of the young people in this study told a story of transit. Whether they moved from other states or merely other schools, these students often began the stories they told of the WELL with movement. It is of note however that these stories were not laments but rather stated somewhat dryly, as if it simply was the way of the world. For example, when asked about himself generally, Jim, a white magnet student, offered:

JIM Uh, I was born in Norfolk, Virginia. My dad was in the Navy and I lived with my dad and my step-mom. I don't know my real mom and I live in Garner [a suburb to the east of Raleigh] right now. Um, I like to follow sports. Um, I'm a fairly good student. I excel in World Civ. and...

Stories of Race and Class: Borders and Border Crossings

Two students, members of the Student Advisory Board to the WELL, talked about the social groups of the school across the street and its effects on the WELL. As every story is a partial story, so too is every story multiple. However, Matthew and Todd do define groups at Holden with great precision. Interestingly, they speak of "downtown people" in very particular ways that, they theorize, relates to racial demographics of the WELL.

MATHEW Do y'all know any like downtown people?

TODD Yeah.

MATHEW They don't come here at all 'cause everybody has that idea—this is where all black people hang out.

R Oh, so—no, wait—hold it. Say that again. The downtown people—what's that?

MATHEW Preps.

R Inside the beltline?

TODD Inside the beltline.

MATHEW Inside the beltline.

TODD Yeah.

MATHEW All that inside the beltline.

R I just—now, downtown means a lot of things to different people, right?

TODD Yeah.

R So downtown people—which are your preps—which means what?

TODD Preps—what else? They all hang out together. They're all the outspoken people. Who all know everyone.

MATHEW He can define it better.

TODD Their parents know everyone.

MATHEW Rich kids. … Definitely rich.

The depiction of this group of students includes many identifiers of note. In geographic terms the first term of "downtown people" obviously refers to a section of Raleigh—confusing at first—that clarifies with the addition of "inside the Beltline," a real estate designation related to property value. These "downtown people" or "preps," as they are referred to in other places in these stories, are the historical student population of Holden, explicitly not magnet students. Of course, many of the students who attend the WELL live "downtown" but not in the neighborhoods that these students associate with the term. This designation is without question both raced and classed. In essence, the phrase "downtown people" in reference to the elite of Holden High School signifies a symbolic ownership of the geographical area, the entire central city. While people of color may inhabit downtown Raleigh, they could never fit into the signifying marker of "downtown people" and, in similar fashion, those students who through magnet status have enrolled at Holden also find a politics of exclusion at work—one based on geography.

Emily, a 16-year-old African-American, began her story with a comparison to another high school she attended—notable in that she was a freshman at the time of the interview, indicating that this was her second high school in her first year. I found Emily on the sidewalk outside the WELL chatting animatedly with a circle of friends. She wore an unopened condom packet inside the lens of her glasses emulating Lisa Left Eye Lopez, a hip-hop artist who took up the cause of sexual heath for young women. I wondered when the condom had been brought out by Emily. Holden, as all schools in this Southern school district, enforced a strict policy of "abstinence only" in terms of sexual health and acceptable topics of conversation between students and teachers. Surely, a display of this brazen would have caused a stir on school grounds but, at this moment, Emily was not technically on school grounds; she, like the smokers on the street corner to the north, stood prominently and defiantly on the border. The sidewalk on Bishop St. is the border between school and the WELL and the students understanding of these spatial distinctions was clear.

The WELL was one of only a few after-school options approved by Emily's group home and she walked the line of compliance with those imperatives. She spent her after-school time at the WELL by skirting the border, moving back and forth across. While one might argue that she was technically following her directive to be at the lab, she certainly was not working on homework or studying on this day. She was both *at* the WELL and *not at* the WELL. This prominently displayed condom seemed to be about playing with borders as well. Certainly, openly sexually charged conversation is transgressive for a 16-year-old girl in adult spaces, yet her immediate explanation of the social cause of "safe sex" makes her hard to chastise. Of course, I am unable to know how her conversation changes when the space becomes a student one through adult absence. Yet her ability to shift and respond to the differing social formations allows her to operate in both. Through this playing with boundaries, she is both transgressive and progressive, all the while with a knowing mischievous smile.

Emily's comments begin with differentiating Holden from another high school (a new one built in a wealthy suburb far to the north of downtown Raleigh) and immediately mentioning race and social hierarchies.

EMILY I enjoy school. I just–I don't like Holden.

R Why not?

EMILY Um, it's too–I don't want to say segregated, but like when I used to go to Forrest [High School]…we were all very diverse. Everyone hangs–like, hung around with everybody.

R What about those groups at Holden?

EMILY Um,…[pause] you're in groups that you're in because of the shoes you wear. There's like the stuff you do after school, how you talk.

R: So… you felt like Forrest was more diverse in terms of who people hung out with.

EMILY Mm-hmm. And I feel the curriculum is better at Forrest too. Emily notes that fashion, after-school activities, and social markers like "how you talk" determine social groupings at Holden High School. Without doubt, these markers operate in ways that are both classed and raced. "The type of shoes you wear" could not only refer to the racial markers in the appropriation of style by different groups but also to the hierarchy of fashion existing in the complex world of brand recognition and the simple elevation of expensive goods. These markers are so clear to Emily that she uses them to describe the WELL in exclusionary terms.

EMILY You can't just take your average preppy rainbow sandal wearing
　　　Caucasian person and bring them over and have them like, 'hey, guys, what are you doing' [in overplayed white dialect]? No, like, when I say, when I say a white person [at the WELL], I mean someone who's been affiliated with colored people all their lives [referring to herself as 'colored' person].

R You see—here at the WELL, do you see very many of your average preppy rainbow sandal wearing white people?

EMILY (laughs as if this is ridiculous)

R All right.

EMILY Um...

R Are they here?

EMILY There's a few. Those are the studious type.

So, for Emily, the "preppy rainbow sandal wearing white person" might venture into the WELL but clearly they are a marginal few and they are "the studious type," a particular grouping of students that stand outside the majority of those who attend. It is probably worth noting that the signifier "rainbow sandal wearing" refers to a particular brand of footwear (actually a flip-flop) that serves to identify what others in course of these conversations have called "downtown people." Rainbow is a trademark, a brand name for a certain series of products that range from $30 to $60—expensive for flip-flops! The style signifies a connection to the beach, or "downeast" as the regional expression goes. The "downtown people" and the wealthy of Raleigh in general, spend a significant number of weekends and the summer at vacation homes on the North Carolina coast. These sandals combined with certain hairstyles and "preppie" fashion are part of the Raleigh "look" for the social elite and associate these certain students with a standard of leisure. They are so valued as a marker of social status that they are often worn even in the dead of winter. Twice in this interview, something as seemingly insignificant as footwear serves to identify the group specifically only marginally apart of the WELL space.

R Okay. Do you feel that race is a problem at the WELL?

EMILY It's not a problem, it's just that, um, I don't like to say what—do I say colored people?

R It doesn't matter. I mean, I think black is fine. African American is fine.

EMILY Oh, I'm not trying to like be racist or anything.

R Say what you mean.

EMILY Okay. I think the African Americans,... they feel like they're higher than Caucasian people because—I remember my first week here, I was walking with a group of black girls and this little white girl was minding her own business and she accidentally bumped into one of them and then all of them got heated and the girl that she bumped into, she was like, "'Excuse me, you bumped into me. Excuse you." And they, they–she was ready to fight because this little girl bumped into her–not, not on purpose–accidentally.

EMILY And this little girl was terrified.

EMILY And, and it's like they, they don't care.

R You don't see that at Forrest?

EMILY No, not at all.

R What do you think is going on there? Were they–were these older girls?

EMILY No, they were like, they were like sophomore–freshman/sophomore girls and stuff like that.

R Hmm.

EMILY And of course, like, 'cause–whenever I bump into someone, I'm like, "Excuse me."

EMILY And then when I saw this, I was like, whoa.

R If you had to guess, what? What do you think is going on there? That sounds weird…'cause you didn't see it at Forrest.

EMILY Yeah, I didn't say–as far as I understand–I said–I don't want [to] say always.

Emily's confusion over raced terms here is an interesting break in the narrative. While she is an African-American (although possibly of mixed racial identity), she struggles to find the correct term for the black girls she goes on to speak about. Perhaps, as her story is one of distancing herself from their behaviors, she stumbles for a term to describe a raced group in the particular place of Holden High School. For her to speak in generalized terms involving racial groupings is awkward but seems to allude to how race is performed within the borders of the school. Related to this social performance of race, how students navigate the hallways of Holden and the ways in which social groups exclude individuals via spaces—in this case using the threat of violence—seem to shock Emily but she stops short of directly calling this part of the race problem at Holden. She states that African-Americans "feel like they're higher than Caucasian people" implying that power—at least in hallway politics—is held by black students. Another interpretation might be that this incident shows a symbolic move to power by a group that, within the acknowledged structure of the school, has none.

Stories of Safety

Jennie, a ninth grade African-American student, describes the WELL as "a safe place," a place where the people are nice and you can get your work done. A regular attendee of the WELL, she situates herself constantly in front of a computer. For her, this place is about homework and email. Bernardo, a Latino staff member, has helped Jennie with her writing assignments and it seems that she now comes to depend on some kindly editing before she turns anything in. But also in Jennie's story is a spatial relationship that speaks to material realities for this young girl. Jennie's brother attends NC State—a mere two blocks away—and helps her mother with transporting Jennie between school and home. This proximity makes this place of help and safety possible. Troubled over riding the bus, she explains that "people be mean" on the bus and quickly refers to fighting on the bus by kids from her neighborhood and in the bus parking lot. For Jennie, this "safe place" provides a solution to a set of fears that she navigates during her time at the high school across the street. Her language is one of opposition, "over there" and "there not here." She sees the crossing of the street to the WELL as a break with those concerns. She and others, "come to get away from trouble."

Jim, a white sophomore, also speaks of safety in his opening remarks about the WELL. As we will see later, Jim enjoys the moments of confrontation that occasionally happen at the WELL, even offering to join in an unclear form of physical regulation of aberrant behavior, but his reasons for attending the WELL reside in fear over issues of bullying.

R Why do you spend time at the WELL?

JIM I spend time at the WELL because my mom doesn't pick me up after school because she doesn't get off until 5:00 and I don't want to ride the bus home. So I can come to the WELL and get some work done if I need it and possibly some help in the subject and I like the people that work here.

R Why don't you ride the bus home?

JIM I'd be the minority. I'd, I'd probably be the—there'd probably be five white people on the bus and I feel uncomfortable. I got, I got bullied by a lot of the—I don't, I don't—I'm not racist. I don't want to come out and say black people, but African-American people are a lot of mean people—when I was in elementary school and I rode the bus, I got bullied. So I just stopped riding it.

R So you think if you just stopped riding the bus you wouldn't be bullied?

JIM Probably not, but I...

R What's interesting about that is—wouldn't you say that it's predominately African-American people who come here [the WELL]?

JIM: Oh, yeah.

R Why doesn't the same thing happen?

JIM You mean...

R You're not getting bullied or...

JIM Oh, no. You can't—if someone messes with me or something, I can just tell Jack and he'll kick them out and that's not—I mean if I bullied a little African-American kid, I'd get kicked out. It's not—it's neutral. But a lot of minorities do come here.

R Is that how—I mean, how is it neutral? How do they, how do they do that when the bus isn't neutral?

JIM Well, um, how, how could—what do you mean?

R Why is this, why is this place safe and other places not?

JIM On the bus, you've got one bus driver who's driving the bus and can't really do anything if someone's getting bullied or someone–but here, you've got like five people on your hand to weight you whenever you need them.

For Jim, the structure of the WELL itself disallows the type of bullying that seemed to have a profound impact on his experiences in elementary school. Jack, the obviously admired assistant director, provides the reassurance that certain behaviors would not be tolerated. Jim's troubling essentialized description of African-Americans as "mean people" was not quite contradicted by the admission that many minorities attend the WELL. Rather, he suggests that the presence of multiple staff members ensures that the inevitable bullying cannot happen in *this* place.

Across these stories, the WELL and the school across the street are always already in relation. The stories they tell jump back and forth across the border, and the particular place that has been made at the WELL allows for a type of reflection as well as analysis on the social relations that mark the day-to-day of the high school. The bus—the most liminal of spaces—is spoken of not just in terms of transition and movement across the city but in terms of safety and vulnerability, a necessary but dangerous part of the life of young people. Again, how the place of the WELL is constructed by these young people provides not only an opportunity to live together otherwise but also opens up the space for a critique.

Stories of Opposition

Two other students tell different stories about the WELL. Sharia, and Ward, also consistent attendees of the WELL, an 11th grade African-American and a 9th grade Asian-American, respectively, represent a different type of WELL kid. These two students are never in front of computers. They are more likely to be out on the front steps if the weather is nice—a practice against the rules but tolerated for certain kids—or down in the study area, leaning in over piles of textbooks and folders, talking intently about *very serious issues*. My interview with them—they insisted on coming together—was frankly, a disappointing one. Our informal conversations on those front steps were complex and reflective musings on both the WELL and the intricacies of that imposing high school across the street. But by the time the interview came around, they were hesitant, reluctant to speak openly as if they were betraying something/someone in participating. Their body language and hesitation felt like an uneasy confession, like they were getting away with something at the WELL and did not want to mess that up.

The interview presented a language of opposition, but of a very different nature than those of others interviewed. Ward and Sharia spoke of their dissatisfaction with the academics across the street. It was clear that they were bored but something about this place provided a possibility for something else. Their responses to the question, why do people come to the WELL, illustrate:

SHARIA some of it is to use the computer...the need to study, but...it's [the WELL] interesting, to get different ideas. The WELL creates an environment where you can say things... [an] atmosphere...teachers aren't breathing down your neck, a safe chaos. It's within some control, you have a choice; school is just going through the motions.

WARD Not for computers. I like some of the people here; here I have someone to talk to.

The critical geography frame is useful here: the comments of the students make clear a distinction between the WELL and school, here and there. The lab is "an environment" where one has choices and "someone to talk to." It is important to note that the students neither deny nor claim to overcome the structures of power at work within the school context. Rather, they suggest that the simple act of crossing the street between the WELL and the school—a type of border crossing—enables them to "get what they need." For Sharia, it's ideas. For Ward it's someone to talk to.

Conclusions/Connections

There is not one story of the WELL, but many. The space of the WELL allowed for students to use it for any number of ways to, as Jennie said, "get what they need." The reasons for the students' initial forays into the WELL varied with individual context but some common themes arose as the stories were collected. As the sections of this chapter illustrate, safety and transit dominated the beginning conversations with students at the WELL. Safety, not surprising in its appearance in interviews with contemporary youth, appeared early on in several of the interviews and was somewhat surprising in the intensity as an issue in which it was felt and expressed. The students marked some spaces as safe and some as unsafe, implying the real skill of knowing which is which. The students' stories of transit speak of both the changing economic context and the effects of a shift to the magnet school designation. Those interviewed for this project had moved, changing schools from suburb to urban or even state to state.

All of the stories of the WELL resonate with a sense of place that is defined by its *not* being Holden High School. Some stories of direct opposition occur while others more closely resemble strategies for succeeding within the rules— academic and social—across the street. Ward and Sharia speak very clearly of their dissatisfaction with the intellectual and social "environment" of Holden and describe the WELL in positive terms replete with student power to define the place, limited adult control, and different rules of interaction. Related to this are the stories of Mathew and Todd who use the place to amass later benefits—cultural capital in the competitive world of college applications. Their stories are explicitly strategic but they betray an underlying logic to the collected stories of the WELL—students used this place to navigate the spaces of school, home, and future; they get what they need.

An undercurrent to the students' stories was a theme of belonging. Whether it is the staff (or unofficial staff) relations that make up the "WELL family," Brian's lament that the WELL is not what it once was, or in Jim's violent reaction to a student transgression of the rules, the stories spoke of a sense of ownership, community, and even a contingent identity. The WELL provided a place for these high school students to fulfill those needs in ways the school across the street obviously did not. Emily's depiction of the social groups of Holden, both raced and classed, illustrated not only the exclusionary character of the structure across the street but also how it had been inverted at the WELL. The "average, Rainbow sandal wearin' white person" is not only absent from the place made by the students at the WELL, but (s)he is also not welcome.

The particular context of Holden High School in the history and socioeconomics of the city of Raleigh serves as the field in which these students and the WELL operate. As pointed out by the students themselves, Holden enjoys a particular reputation in the city based on its historical prominence as a public school and as the school for the elite of Raleigh. As shifts in the demographics of the city changed and educational policy came to allow, Holden became a magnet school in order to attract students outside their traditional districting. The students interviewed and observed in this study live with and comment on a school that has changed as the school population has changed, and as the city itself has undergone the transformations of late capitalism. The spatial dynamics of the WELL are presented as deeply entangled in the politics of the school across the street. This relational understanding of the two places resembles more of a negotiated set of meanings as opposed to resistance or rejection (remember that participation in the WELL was entirely voluntary). Issues of race and class permeate both spaces, but the students felt much more comfortable with how those concerns could be addressed at the WELL. Issues of belonging and identity worked in fundamentally different ways within the new context of a changing school dynamic but the stories presented here are attempts to begin to understand those differences.

In spending time with the students at the WELL, layers of the map begin to come into focus. The answer to why students spent time at the WELL revealed itself to be complex and, at times contradictory as stories of safety, stories of change, border stories, and stories of opposition all co-exist for the students of this place. Taking space seriously in this analysis opened up the possibility for reflection and even critique of the experiences of these young people but notably does so in material, affective, and discursive ways. The material spaces both close off and open up potentiality for ways of being/knowing/doing (Gershon

2017) for the youth represented here. This enabled a more capacious analysis that includes the understandings that affect can be described if not fully known, discourse can be troubled and stumbled over, and identity can be seen as work in progress: becoming. The curriculum of the WELL contains a multiplicity of negotiated and/or rejected intentions and the project of coming to understand these striations calls for a present, embodied interaction with the youth that take up the work of this particular place-making. Bringing Critical Geography into conversation with curriculum theory points to new aspects of "the lived experience of school" as it privileges the ways in which school and other spaces are in relation, not bounding the object of analysis but reveling in complex, fluid assemblages that make up the process of place-making. What this approach provides is not only a look into what traditional curriculum theorizing would call the null curriculum (i.e., what is taught by not teaching it) but instead introduces the spaciocurricular—the consideration of *what is taught where*.

Notes

1   The term "New South" first refers to a slogan used after the Civil War as part of reform efforts focusing on the shift from an agrarian to industrial economy, a modernization of southern society, and more integrated relationship with the United States as a whole. In more contemporary times, the term signifies the period of economic and financial sector growth in cities like Atlanta, Charlotte, Dallas-Fort Worth, and Raleigh-Durham.

2   Some proper names of places and persons that might compromise participant anonymity have been changed to pseudonyms for the purpose of this study. Additionally, although the WELL still exists it has significantly shifted its structure and operation. As a result, it will be referred to here in the past tense to represent its nature from 1996 to approximately 2004.

3   Wozolek (2021) importantly conceptualizes affect "both as it travels in, between, and through human bodies and as a set of complex intentions between human and non-human bodies" (p.14). Only recently have I turned to Affect Theory and its potentiality for thinking through spaciocurricular analysis.

3

SPACES OF POSSIBILITY

Stepping into the space of the WELL opened up a new, vibrant geography but it resonated with familiar tones. As a teacher at the high school across the street before starting my PhD work, I began to think about the spatiality of my school, my classroom, and what all of those things might mean. First, I thought about my classroom, tucked up on the 3rd floor and on a row of classroom that were primarily for special education. I liked being isolated as I took an approach to teaching that was something like us vs. them, meaning me and the students were together against everyone else who didn't understand. I thought of myself as a radical educator and, true or not, I openly encouraged students to think of the four walls of my classroom as a different kind of space, one in which the other constraints, or labels, or reputations outside of it didn't matter. I didn't call it a space of possibility then, but it would seem that this is what I was hoping to create. Some success was evidenced by what started happening during lunch. A few of my students asked if they could eat lunch in my room, explaining that the lunchroom wasn't safe for them (their word). I said yes and it became a thing. Soon, however, it wasn't just my students coming to my room at lunch; students came that I didn't recognize in specific but I did in general. What I mean is that I saw kids that didn't fit the norm of the high school social scene—it was hip hop kids, goth kids, punk/redneck kids, gay kids, nerdy kids all mixed together. These were the kids that didn't fit in and they were looking for spaces where they could bring and be who they were, even if just for lunch. One could say a lot about the geographies of lunchrooms, bathrooms, and hallways in schools but what I saw up close was simply young people working out ways to navigate and negotiate school spaces with interludes of places where they could be themselves. Truth be told, I didn't like the lunchroom or, God forbid, the teachers lounge either as I felt like I was still on duty or out of place yet again. I came to learn that my classroom was on the special education hall because I was considered "special ed friendly," something of which I was proud but also saddened in the implication that many of my colleagues were not. I begin this chapter with these reflections as they mark how we bring ourselves into spaces, ourselves in process and in contradiction. The placemaking we undertake involves those selves and their embodied histories, economies, and affects. There are internal geographies here. In classrooms, students and teachers alike weave themselves into spaces and co-construct what they might mean. Whether in solidarity or not, in intention or not, they always already do this in relation. There are possibilities here.

Geographies are often first thought of in terms of the physical environment—rivers, valleys, lakes, mountain chains, and the like—and certainly the interaction of the human and non-human world holds a great deal of potential for inquiry. Cities, towns, and communities too can be simply thought of as naturally bounded, timeless—as they've always been. A critical geography disrupts these tendencies and provokes a deeper analysis, a consideration of the ways in which history, culture, the affective, and the socio-economic work on these spaces and create the ground on which humans begin their constant negotiation with that non-human world. The realization that these intra-actions (i.e., the co-constitutive nature of an entangle agency; see Barad 2007) are not *a priori*, predetermined or neutral opens up a curricular question: what do these spaces try to teach us? Further, interior geographies of human constructed spaces also evidence flows of power dynamics. These are socio-material landscapes that both encourage and hinder certain behaviors, which are the physical manifestation of beliefs, norms, and affects. Often, it is these interpersonal spaces where we can see how forces like racism, sexism, homophobia, classism, ableism, and the like land on bodies. The questions of who belongs where, as well as who gets to decide and police those borders, can certainly be found in classrooms, bathrooms, school busses, schools, and other educative spaces like the WELL. Bodies inhabit spaces and, therefore, the social constructs that divide, marginalize, empower, and oppress are all spatialized. Part of the inquiry here then includes thinking through what these spaces are trying to teach us and in what ways are those efforts to teach us spatialized; this is what I call the *spaciocurricular*.

Tightening the aperture of our analysis further, this chapter explores the spaces of the WELL in what feminist geographer Leslie Kern—following poet Adrienne Rich—calls "'the geography closest in,' the body and everyday life" (2020, p. 7). At the WELL, differences in how students identify with the place got complicated as some "regulars" often referred to less enthusiastic participants in the culture of the place as "buspass kids" (i.e., they were only there for the free bus pass). The youth who spend time at the WELL all reflect some alienation from the race and social class dynamics across the street at the high school but the sorting and sifting of the social in this place is no less complicated. Some students would also serve as staff members and often reached that position through being a regular attendee and eventually being offered the job. Something was clearly happening with place and identity here and questions arose as to what this place was teaching the students who spent time there and what identity work did this place enable, hinder, or complicate? How did the geographies of the WELL work on the interior geographies of these students?

Community and Confrontation

...the WELL family

I attended a staff meeting in which the group described their work as having two main components: to "Enforce Rules" and "Empower the Students." Jack, a white 19-year-old and the only full-time staffer at the WELL, makes both, perhaps contradictory, comments enthusiastically and the group hastily nods agreement. Jack was the original staff member when the lab first opened and has continued to work beyond his graduation from Holden High School. Not only does he technically have authority over the other staff members but he has come to somewhat represent "the staff" in the minds of the kids who attend and work there. Often in interviews and casual conversations "staff" and Jack are used interchangeably. This is to say that if the staffers disagree with a point made in this interchange, it would be unlikely that it would be challenged with Jack there. However, Jack seems to truly believe the rhetoric of the WELL and sees himself as living proof of its potential for redirecting young people. He is funny, confident, and charismatic; it is no wonder why he is popular with students and adults alike. Jack, in an interview, continues his explication of the purposes of the WELL in what seem to be phrases often heard and often quoted.

JACK our goal is to bridge the 'cyber-gap' and provide a 'happy learning environment' [making gestures in the air denoted quotations]...we want to see students heading in the right direction. The students here are always doing something new... it's inspiring as a student to see other students learning.

R How does this place work?

JACK it's the rapport that you build with the students.

BERNARDO [AGREEING] if you're nice to us, we're nice to you.

Although they agree, Jack and Bernardo approach their work at the WELL differently perhaps in large part due to their different roles. While once Jack would have been the staffer assigned to handing out bus passes, now he plays more of a management role. He delegates such tasks to the other staffers—like Bernardo or Matt—and portrays himself as a mentor to the younger staff members. He began as student that found the WELL to be a place in which he could excel, he moved to staff working with younger students, and now, as a college student has moved to position himself as a mentor to other staffers. The geography of the WELL, with its openness to possibility in this space, has allowed him this degree of movement.

The use of air quotes by Jack in reference to the "cyber-divide" and "happy learning environments" indicates a certain savvy to the multiple discourses at work at the WELL. Jack hears the education lingo in board meetings and conversations with faculty and other adults in reference to the work at the WELL but seems to imply that something else is actually going on. In my time interviewing and observing at the lab, I was surprised to learn that most of the students who regularly attend (and agreed to talk to me) actually did have access to computers at home and came for different reasons. Jack knows more about why students come than most but is intelligent enough to know that the official rhetoric for this place's existence is slightly different. My sense is that he was letting me know that he knows about both the real story and the story he's supposed to tell.

Bernardo, however, sees himself as something of a gatekeeper to this space. He relishes his role as "enforcer"—a term used by more than one staffer to refer to his role. Bernardo, a Latino 10th grader frequently wearing a Clash t-shirt and a slight punk rock aesthetic (meaning an unimposing studded bracelet or a slight rip in the jeans or shirt) states his role in a way that emphasizes his authority, "if you're nice to us, we're nice to you" and, referring to the distribution of bus passes, "sometimes they try to fool me." But perhaps more telling than Bernardo's identification with power is his use of the collective pronouns "us" and "we." This power that he has identified with is a collective one; the staff (and those that flirt with the distinction) see themselves, at least in the specific place of the WELL, as a group.

In my time at the WELL there was often talk of fights and what the students call "drama," but, as was my experience in classrooms, one rarely saw it in the extreme. Fights and physical confrontations tend to take on a mythic quality with students; the tales of the fight and the fighters travel fast and quickly become exaggerated with the telling. Actually, I never saw anything I would call serious. There were kids asked to leave—who generally made a mumbling but compliant exit—and there were voices raised on occasion, but it was quite notable that generally the peace was maintained with what seemed to be little effort.

There was however an interesting event during my interview with Jim, who was there every day that I was. It was clear that the WELL was an important part of his day. Jim spent his time interacting with the staff, hanging around with them (even in the supposed restricted areas of the front steps and back office). It seemed that Jim saw himself as if not part of the staff, but definitely the next rung on the ladder of authority. Jim eagerly volunteered for an interview about the WELL, so much so that I treat his comments with a little skepticism—his comments in places sound a little like the "party line." Our interview was interrupted by Mark, a staff member and junior at Holden, who I think came to tell me about the confrontation but quickly gets wrapped up in an interrogation by Jim.

MARK So y'all missed another confrontation.
R I missed a fight?
MARK It's a buspass kid from like last week when he...
R Where? Is he still here?
MARK No, I kicked him off. He was getting...
JIM Is he outside? Can I see him?
MARK No, he left.

JIM What's he look like?

MARK Uh, he's just a little punk.

JIM Why didn't you come get me?

MARK I told you.

R You haven't had trouble with him before?

MARK Well, Steve did and he tried to come back today and I…

JIM [excitedly interrupting] If you see him walk by, come get me.

MARK He come walking in the lab. I was like, I was like, you can't be here.

JIM Dude, I would have picked him up and slammed him.

MARK You can't be here. He was like, "I didn't do anything, man." He kept on walking. So I was like, here we go again. So he just kept on runnin'…you know, runnin' his mouth. And other little things—yo, yo, yo, you're…

JIM I would have slammed him.

MARK He was like, "You'd better be glad there's cameras in here." I'm like, dude, just let it go.

R That's what he said? 'You'd better be glad there's cameras?'[1]

MARK Uh-huh. So we went outside, and he's like…

JIM Dude, why didn't you come get me, man? (pleading tone)

MARK 'Cause, I mean…

JIM I could have done something.

MARK And then Jack came and he was still running his mouth and I'm like, dude, just leave. It's not that difficult.

R He wanted a bus pass?

MARK Yeah, he's like, he's like, how am I going to get home? And I was like, well, that's not my concern. You know he wanted bus pass. How you get home is however you figure out how to get home.

JIM What's he look like?

MARK It's not my problem. Amy [a staff member] gave him a bus pass and so I was like…

JIM Somehow, I bet she is [implying that Amy will still give a bus pass to the offending individual].

MARK No she's not! 'Cause I'm going to do bus passes today. You can only get one anyways. It's not like she—'cause if she needs one, then…

JIM What's that dude look like?

MARK Huh? What's he look—he's got earrings, doo-rag. He's probably about this tall, skinny, uh. He's African-American. I'm not worried about it, but I'm going to let y'all get back to y'all's thing.

JIM All right.

R Why are you so concerned about that? You just want to see something exciting?

JIM Yeah, I'm not an instigator, but I, I'll admit, I like drama.

R (laughs) Tell me about the drama at the WELL.

JIM Well, unfortunately, I'm never here to see it. I always miss it.

R Like me.

JIM But, uh, I'm very nosy when it does happen–when a student refuses to leave–mainly that's pretty much always the case.

There's a lot going on in the above interview. Jim seemed overly interesting in this story of a transgression of the WELL rules (even to staff member Mark who seems puzzled by the intensity of his questions). For Jim, the ability to kick someone out of the WELL defines authority at the WELL and a distinction between simply student, universally under adult control, and student staff member who enjoys a degree of power. Jim offers to "slam" the offending student—an offer, to a staff member no less, in flagrant opposition to rules about violence at the WELL—in a show of bravado that feels like a hesitant offer for initiation. Further, the young men eventually define the problem as a failure on the part of the only female staff member, Amy. The offending student, apparently appeased with a bus pass in the past by Amy, returned expecting the same treatment from Mark. Interestingly, Jim not only reinforces that the problem lies with Amy but pushes it further leading to an analysis of his statements toward a gender critique. What is clear is that the students at the WELL feel protective about the place they have made there. They care about the place, are invested in maintaining it, and relate it to a broader sense of self, an identity. The transgression here was in crossing the border where one did not belong, noted by not following the rules, although the creation and communication of those rules seems ambiguous and perhaps serve as their own marker of position within the structure of the WELL. The social categories of "WELL kid" vs. "buspass kid" are marked clearly and signify differing inner geographies, differing relations with place itself—maps of meaning that highlight the intra-action of bodies and places.

Filling up space

The two young men who served on the Student Advisory Board (SAB) commenting on the different groups of students who spend time at the WELL noted that some students seem to simply need a place to wait for their parents. The "sanctuary"—notably, I only heard this foyer referred to in this way by these two—is a small waiting room outside the offices of the Director and the Office Manager. Below the computer lab, it lies somewhat between the formal study room and the business of the two offices and feels like a "waiting room." It also happened to be outside where the interviews were taking place and the laughter and voices sometimes distracted us from our conversation. The two young men seemed perturbed that we were being distracted but they seemed to apply their frustration to issues of the WELL in general. One of the groups they identified at the WELL was characterized by them in the following way:

TODD The black guys in the sanctuary who just need to fill up their time.
MATHEW Yeah.

R I don't understand 'the sanctuary.'

TODD you know, 'a sanctuary'–that's the little thing.

R Is that what that is over there?

TODD Yeah, that's what that is–right where the guys are just sitting out there laughing.

R Right.

TODD Yeah, they're just filling up that space.

MATHEW Yeah, and like their parents come…

TODD They're there every day. Yeah, their parents will come get them.

The foyer is called "the sanctuary" because of the medieval paintings on the wall (Steve, the director, is a medievalist and remnants of that interest can be found scattered around the WELL). These students, named "black boys" by the two in the interview, need to "fill up time" so they end up "just filling up that space." In effect however, these students have negotiated the systems and structures of the WELL to find a *place*—as it has meaning to them and notably not to the students interviewed—that allows for social interaction only occasionally under adult or staff scrutiny, the scrutiny literally "passes by" on the way to something else (the lab, the study room, the office, etc.). Coded understandings of place and race seem to run through this narrative and the stories that follow; but in considering Wozolek's reminder that "place is a process, something made rather than incidentally formed, the places and spaces that students of color negotiate can be understood as a margin that is a purposefully designed and designated position" (2015, p. 26), it would be inappropriate to accept the idea that the black students were only filling up space. Their own negotiation of the space of the WELL, and the intra-action of the high school across the street open up the possibilities of resistance and resilience as much as any other student there.

When asked about the perception of the WELL among their peers at Holden, these two students—who are white and see themselves as unique in their participation at the WELL—describe how race is involved in the characterization of the WELL space. Their friends and acquaintances use "they" to racially code the WELL as black and then attach to it the stereotypes held by them.

R Okay, now they, they what? What was the statement?

MATHEW Well, I know, like I was–yeah, they just kind of have like this thing that all the black people–they don't have anything to do–hang out here. And this–I'm not joking. I have like a direct quote… I mean, like I, I took these SAT classes and there was like a couple of people that I did know from Holden and, you know, they were pretty much downtown people.

They were pretty–yeah, they were all downtown people, but–and, you know, I was just kind of like, hey, I went to–I was telling them about my camping trip that

I went with the WELL and just kind of had this like little, you know, face expression like, 'whoa, what are you doing hanging out with those guys?,' you know?

Here the students start to mark the student population spatially—"downtown people" refers to the neighborhoods surrounding Holden High School. As detailed in the previous chapter, this group historically has been the white population served by the school and still holds a prominent position in the school hierarchy. These neighborhoods straddle the oak tree lined streets passed on our metaphorical drive into this city. These two students are peers of the "downtown people" but clearly separate themselves from that group. Their participation in the activities of the WELL not only set them apart but evidence a different of preconception that opened up the space of the WELL as a one of possibility for these two students. In the interview, Mathew explains with the affirmation of Todd.

MATHEW And even one of my friends does that too—Kelly.

TODD Huh?

MATHEW Kelly.

TODD Oh, yeah, yeah, yeah.

MATHEW Like I mean she's downtown... And like she just has this–when you say something about the WELL, they kind of have this like, you know, I thought all the, you know, dorks or people that don't have anything to do hang out there.

TODD Those are all the downtown people [that] just don't come here really.

MATHEW Yeah, unless they're forced to by a teacher or like, like, you know, a projector something.

TODD They're not like afraid to come here. Like, oh, man, those black people at the WELL are going to bully us, but it's not like they're going to have a problem. They just don't come here because...

MATHEW Because the majority of the people here are...

TODD Yeah, they're mostly black people.

MATHEW That's the same thing. Like if in the beginning–I guess when the WELL started, if a lot of downtown people came here, you wouldn't see a lot of black people here.

TODD Yeah.

MATHEW But I guess the black people started coming here and that's why you don't see downtown people. I mean, it's not like bad I guess 'cause I'm pretty sure they could find [places that are]...

TODD ... Racially diverse [Todd finishes Mathew's statement].

MATHEW I mean, I'm pretty... [doesn't finish thought]

TODD Well, you're lacking the majority.

MATHEW Yeah.

TODD And you would think... what is it? Like 80 percent should be white and 20 percent should be black. Okay it should be 70/30 and the population is more like 90/10. I mean–I don't know... There may not be that–it's probably 80/20, but it's not 70/30–in reverse!

MATHEW Yeah (laughs). It is.

It should be noted here that although Mathew and Todd are members of the SAB, during my time at the WELL I did not see much of them. They certainly didn't spend their time behind the computers in the lab. If they were around, they would occupy those places of privilege—that connoted some status—like behind the front desk (although they did not work there) or the front steps with staff members. Also, my observations characterized the WELL as being much more "racially diverse," in Todd's terms, than the two boys describe. It seems that although the two have used the WELL "to get what they need" and challenge the stereotypical view of the WELL held at Holden High School, the perception that this facility is an African-American space still holds.

TODD Those that–those white people that are here are mostly like the people that–those who work here, like me. I know people who work here and I come talk to the people that work here–like, Jeff... [for example, a student I did not meet in my time at the WELL]

MATHEW Yeah.

TODD He used to come here every afternoon like I did, then–now, he can drive and so, he parks here. That's how a bunch of the white people come here. I mean–I don't know.

For Todd, it is necessary to highlight the reasons that white people come to the WELL. Clearly, for him, the introduction of white people into a black space requires some explaining. He mentions "white people" specifically three times in rapid succession to emphasize his point that this is an unusual phenomenon. To further understand his own positioning in participation at the WELL, how he initially describes himself reveals important distinctions between himself and other "white people" at Holden. Todd notes a transactional relationship between some students and the WELL, one that perhaps shifts over time but, again, race and class seem to be undercurrents within these intra-actions.

TODD Uh, I'm a junior at Holden and I've been here all three years. I'm a magnet student, uh...

R Which means?

TODD Which means...

MATHEW [interrupting] it's really far to his house.

TODD Yeah and I drive myself 'cause I'm not in this school district.

R Mm-hmm. Yeah.

TODD Uh, I don't know. I'm in the Student Advisory Board and Key Club. I don't play any sports.

R Okay.

MATHEW I'm a junior too, at [Holden] and, uh, I'm not a magnet student (laughs).and I'm in SAB, that's why I'm here at the WELL and I get a ride from Todd.

R So be careful about the bus cracks

MATHEW Yeah, yeah.

R Since he's your ride [laughs].

Ways of Belonging

> ...it lets you join into the family

Mathew and Todd, two white members of the SAB, comment on issues of inclusion and exclusion at the WELL. They are unable to describe their involvement at the WELL—particularly the SAB—without referring to the structure of extracurricular activities across the street at Holden. When asked about their own reasons for participating in activities at the WELL, the answer begins in definitive terms regarding college applications but evolves into a deeper concern for relationships that are formed within the activities both at the WELL and in other settings, referred to as being part of the "WELL family."

MATHEW It looks good on your college application. That's why I'm doing it 'cause I haven't really joined any clubs. So this is why I'm doing this. You'll be going on trips and camping.

TODD Obviously it looks great for college [which is] for about anyone pretty much their number one goal in high school. There's a couple of real genuinely nice people [at the WELL], but on the most part–I mean, they could enjoy it, but still with that, that was at least what brings you to it. But I think once you're in it then you kind of get the, uh–you kind of get to be part of the WELL family kind of thing. I don't know if they said anything about–I don't know.

R It's come up. [notably by adults in most cases]

TODD Yeah.

R I'm not sure if I'm clear on what that means, but...

TODD Well, most–all of the people who work here are–or I get the impression that they're pretty much like a family. They just hang out all the time.

MATHEW Yeah.

TODD You, you can treat them just like a family. You know, you can tell them anything and, you know, they just have a good time together just like the WELL goes on trips all the time and...

MATHEW It's not just, it's not just a Student Advisory Board. It's the whole WELL.

TODD Well, no, they used–they go on staff trips all time, but once the Student Advisory Board tried to get going a little bit, then we went on a Student

Advisory Board trip, but all the WELL staff went. So it was kind of–it lets you join into the family and you kind of feel like you're part of that group.

The term "WELL family" refers to this extra- extracurricular piece to the experience of this place. Some students and staff have embarked, with the encouragement and guidance of the director Steve, on excursions outside the bounds of this particular urban geography. Most notably, the group has gone on several camping trips where bonding seems to take on deeper levels among those who go. As the previous interaction points out, the students are unclear about how one comes to be invited to the camping trips, and by extension into the WELL family. The boundary between staff and SAB is blurry at best as many SAB members have at one time or another been staff and some members of the staff participate in the activities of the SAB. Also, some individuals like Ward (the Asian-American most often seen with Sharia, as discussed in Chapter 2) seem to be officially in neither group but are able to be involved in all the activities.

...this is where I differ

Amy, one of two female staffers, speaks of motives and concerns related to participating at the WELL. When asked why she chose to become active in the facility's various functions she responded with a telling, "this is where I differ." In her mind, the rest of the staff holds different values and concerns than she does and hints at the gendered dynamics of the WELL family. Like most of them, she was recruited to help with the summer program for incoming freshman but for her that experience helped to form her conception of what she might accomplish by working at the WELL.

AMY when you see freshman come through here, most people on the staff didn't care...for all the students I bicker about, I like being known as the nice person... [I want to show the younger students] stuff to make their lives a little easier [and I am here to] make an impact on people.

Amy sees her work at the WELL as a way in which to help younger students, presumably with skills in information technology and the management of homework assignments. It is important to note that at the time of this interview, Amy was merely a sophomore—one year older than the young students she speaks about so matronly. Amy sees herself as more compassionate and mature than the "boys" of the staff and speaks of her involvement at the WELL in moral terms, laden with social responsibility and perhaps hinting at a gendered sense of self. Her introduction to the WELL, besides her own freshman program, was through a reciprocal tutoring arrangement with Bernardo, another staffer. Bernardo helped Amy with her Spanish homework, while Amy helped him with Honors English. It was through their choice of workspace—easy as Bernardo already worked at the lab—that she came to be a part of the staff.

...it's the only place I could go

Lily, a white 9th grader with braces and a very slight stature, is a regular. She is one of the students who is typically not only in front of a computer monitor but also very conscious of the social scene happening all around her. She pays particular attention to the staff members, almost all male and usually a few years older than she. When approached about doing an interview, Lily was researching online for information on Kurt Cobain (the influential guitarist/songwriter of the grunge rock band Nirvana whose fame became cultish upon his suicide). When asked about herself, Lily lists a common string of identifiers for high school students— "I'm a 9th grader, volleyball player... I do pretty well in school...I have good friends." Although she has good friends at school, here interactions at the WELL seem to be largely about breaking into new social circles. Her responses to the interview questions differ in some ways from the norm as her experiences of other schools, other places inform her understanding of both the WELL and Holden High School.

R Why do you come to the WELL?
LILY [my] parents work and the bus doesn't go to Trinityville... [I] can do homework, check email, read a book...it's the only place I could go. I would
probably have to stay with a teacher if I didn't come to the WELL.

Lily mentions a math teacher that might be an alternative to coming to the WELL but she clearly feels that this is the best of few options. Trinityville, where Lily lives, is a township north of Holden that borders the northern edge of the county. Now, as a result of urban sprawl characteristic of the New South, the once distinct community can be characterized as a suburb of Raleigh and Lily's attendance at Holden High School a direct result of its recent magnet status.

Lily's reasons for attending the WELL diverge from what she sees as the main reasons others attend. Her perspective focuses on the technology available at the WELL while still recognizing the social aspects to the place. Interestingly however is Lily's recognition of the economics of information technology and her unique relationship to it.

R Why do others come to the WELL?
LILY [people] can hang out, friends...email, maybe they don't have a computer
at home, you can print for free [she points out that the library charges by the
page for printing]... you can do homework.
R Why do you think most people come?
LILY Most hang out with friends...[to use] internet and chat

R Tell me about the technology here.

LILY I can't use the internet at home…my dad or sister is always online…[there is] good software here…fast internet connection [mentions the superiority of a T1 line to dialup]…[one can] scan pictures.

When asked about her own relationship to technology, she describes herself as "pretty good at it" as a result of computer classes in middle school and "always ahead of the class" in regards to technology. Lily shifts to talk about her position at the WELL as something of a teacher, a more experienced guide to the students she finds at the WELL.

LILY I help other people here…[I] taught people PowerPoint

She mentions that she would consider joining the staff if it didn't conflict with her volleyball practice during the season. The staff members are clearly the group she identifies with both in terms of a degree of tech savvy and a rock and roll aesthetic. "Cool!" is the response given by Bernardo when he sees that Lily is working on a paper on Kurt Cobain; she is clearly pleased by this.

On the day Lily agrees to do an interview, the interaction with Bernardo evolves into flirtation. Beginning with some gentle mockery, the young man continues to joke with Lily regarding her work who then pretends to be upset by this attention. Eventually, seemingly unconcerned that I am sitting next to her, a raucous grabbing and subsequent tug-of-war with Lily's paper takes place. Having taught high school, this interaction was not surprising except that it seemed out of place here. Also, it is significant to note, that on the staff, Bernardo is known as "the enforcer" and sometimes criticized for being too strictly tied to the rules of acceptable behavior and sometimes getting carried away with his authority. Here, the rules of behavior are clearly contradictory and contextual, applying differently to people in different positions. The flirtation, which can be translated as sexual politics, indeed comes up more than once as a space of contradiction in the actions of the staff. The contradiction between this story and Jim's excitement about the possibility of punishing a rule breaker shows that these social rules are highly contextual and matter differently when different folks are involved. Part of this sense of place is a rather fluid understanding of rules and the role they play in how the young people understand their position within the WELL. Elsewhere, I have argued that this is "a curriculum of no curriculum" and that identity work is taken up by the folks who spend time at the WELL within an economy of interests (Helfenbein, 2005). The curriculum of no curriculum teaches that these types of fluid social relations are possibilities within the spatial confines of the WELL and that there remains room for new configurations and possibilities. However, these spaces of possibility cannot be guaranteed to be positive as those same contradictions may not serve everyone equally well, may serve to marginalize some, and may prove difficult to understand and navigate. What does remain positive, however, is the room provided for young people to negotiate their relationship to the space and the clear demarcation between this space of possibility as opposed to the much stricter constraints of the school across the street.

...in the mix

TODD For one, I come by here every day, so I don't have to make a special trip to go talk to other–well, I don't know any of the–like I already know the people who work here. I know Steve real well and Bart, you know, so it's not like I've got to get along with a whole new group of people that I don't really feel comfortable saying–you know, you might not feel comfortable saying what you want to say.

R Mm-hmm.

TODD And to them, I can't really tell them, hey, this is what's going on and this is what needs to happen ...all that kind of stuff is already known. So it's kind of the convenience and–I don't know, like, one, I could be part of the... I could be an officer in this. Which there's already kind of people in other clubs who are kind of established in there.

MATHEW Yeah.

TODD So, I'll be–you know, like I don't want to stomp on their turf. Well, there was no one's turf to stomp on here. This was opening, so I wanted to help before–you know, help them bring it up along and, you know, I could fill my place high and not stomp on anyone's toes.

R Right, right. Kind of right place, right time?

TODD Right.

When Todd says, "I could be part of the... I could be an officer in this," the distance he feels from the student structure of Holden High School is palatable. He, self-described as a "magnet student," finds himself out of the social networks necessary to work his way up to leadership in a school sponsored club. The physical distance of his home has precluded the types of connections he might need to find success in these endeavors. Significant here is that Mathew, Todd's friend and a new participant in the WELL activities, is not a "magnet kid" but clearly holds Todd to be a close friend and even model (throughout the interview, Todd does most of the talking while Mathew tends to serve as an affirming second voice). For Todd, the welcoming nature of the WELL allowed him easy access to not only a social group but a needed accolade for his college application packet.

MATHEW Yeah, he [Todd] is in the mix.

R He is?

TODD I can't really describe it...they [meaning the students of the WELL] appreciate your differences too.

MATHEW Yeah, they do.

TODD And it's not like you want to be like everyone else. It's, it's such a weirdly diverse group to where like it's good for you to have something about you

that's just so different from everyone else just because that's how–like everyone is very distinctly different.

MATHEW Yeah, see, that's what–that's the deal with other clubs because you see
only like some, like some type of people.

TODD Yeah.

MATHEW Like all the smart people go to one club or–I mean, I'm just saying
like that's how it is.

TODD The Asian Club or...

MATHEW Exactly.

TODD The French Club–just groups like that and there's nothing that says, 'oh,
you have to be this to be in it.' You don't have to be Asian. You don't have to
speak French or anything like that. It's anyone so we have a weird mix of–
not weird, a very diverse mix.

MATHEW I mean [pause] people can do that. They're not going to stop you or
anything, but it just feels weird and this just kind of feels like...

TODD You're already *at the place* [emphasis mine].

MATHEW Yeah.

TODD So you don't start *out of place* [emphasis mine].

MATHEW Yeah.

TODD They're interested if–they're like, whoa, you know if you're different and
they ask you about that and wow, that's pretty cool.

MATHEW Yeah.

R So, it's almost like it's a priority?

TODD Huh? Yeah.

MATHEW Oh, yeah.

TODD It's to have something...It's like this is... outsiders kind of thing. It's like
you, you hit Holden first and you–it's obviously all the other choices are out
there and you don't want to really have to–you don't want the stress of trying to get in that and trying to be like everyone else and you come here and
they invite the different. And you're like, oh, I'm kind of here alone and they
just pull you in like you're one of them from the beginning.

MATHEW Yeah.

TODD It's just like, oh, you're different, but that's fine. It's interesting. So it just
kind of sucks you in.

MATHEW Pretty much and even like other clubs, there's so many people. Like
each club has like 40 or 50 people, you know, and like too many–and like
here, when we only have like what, 20 people...

TODD Right, but I know everyone's name and what...

MATHEW Yeah, so if you go to like any other club and you have no idea and
you're just kind of like in the corner just sitting there. Wow, can't wait to get
out here.

So what then is meant by Todd when he says, "You're already *at the place*. So you
don't start *out of place*" [emphasis mine]? It seems that these two are not only

referencing the physical constraints of the high school (i.e., the size of student groups, the convenience of the WELL, and even parking issues) but extending their commentary into issues of inclusion and exclusion. This serves to emphasize how the rules regarding social groups operated differently across the street from the high school. Being "in the mix" and in the family offered a sense of place that provided the opportunity to renegotiate these relationships. Although clearly, there is ambiguity and perhaps clumsy attempts at the remapping, we can see the possibility in spaces such as these. As they say, being different at the WELL was valued and even expected by the students who congregate there socially. It should be noted that Mathew and Todd were interested in the social capital gained by having membership in a student club on their college application. They used the WELL and their participation in it to further their educational goals, as stated previously to "get what they need" but we see further nuance and the complexities of these intra-actions as part of the allowances of being "in the mix."

Conclusions/Connections

What can be seen in the stories presented here are the contours of the assemblage that makes up the interactions of place, power, affect, and identity at this after-school computer lab. Whether it be a story of community, a story of confrontation, of being in the mix, or the only place possible, students understood this place as one in which the otherwise *was* possible. Beginning with the internal geographies of bodies in intra-action with the material space of the lab opens up a way to see these contours in their fluid, sometimes contradictory, and indeterminate process. The spaciocurricular in this case points to how an openness in the bounds of behavior creates these spaces of possibility enabling broader identity work and new social structures. The roles played by the students within these stories both mimic and contest the traditional social roles and ways of belonging reinforced in the school across the street. I would argue that what is important about the place is in what it enables, what it makes possible.

The ways in which the students' talked race in my interactions with them served as an exemplar of the possibilities of this place. Something was happening at the WELL that allowed for a deeper, critical conversation around the raced and classed realities of these students. In my time at the WELL, I overheard students in intense and critical conversations regarding social class, cliques and bullying, sexuality, *and* race. I suggest that students coming together from this diversity of trajectories to engage in critical (although not always positive) discourse marked the place of the WELL as a unique one. In my experience as a high school educator, these very different students would rarely, if ever, be seen interacting across these socially constructed borders. The space of the WELL enabled this type of border crossing—contingent though it may be—and thus I came to see it as a space of possibility. Spaces of possibility became a marker for my work after this study of WELL in the sense that if I could find this one, surely others were out there.

The stories presented here suggest several things about youth and the practice of making place. The ways in which the students and staff have made place at the William Edenton Learning Lab begin to point to the multiplicity insisted upon by critical geographers. Many different stories can be told about places (Harvey, 1996) and surely the stories told here were influenced in large part by my own position as a researcher and as a former Holden teacher. The spatial analysis here marks the opening steps of the journey of thinking about how students, teachers, and communities navigate the forces acting upon them and subsequently make place—a move toward a critical geography. This parallels work by queer and feminist geographers who leverage the term "world-making" in their analyses. Kern (2020) states that "world-making means the process of both imagining and creating space(s) where things can unfold *otherwise*" (p. 57, emphasis original). The spaces that enable or limit efforts at world-making are distributed unevenly and in transitory, fluid ways: this is the spaciocurricular.

Taken together, these two chapters suggest three aspects of the ways in which young people and educative spaces interact within the changing context of American schooling and the social milieu. First and perhaps least surprising is the affirmation that adults—educators, policy makers, and even researchers—generally do not listen to youth or pay attention to the ways in which they make meaning. These chapters highlight another set of examples in which youth are silenced and ignored but more importantly provides a glimpse into the ways in which students make places in which to critique and express those situational relations. Youth engage in these struggles in complex, and nuanced ways and, as shown here, can include transactional relationships, fluid relationships, and understandings of power relationship, and failed attempts at inclusion. Secondly, this study of the WELL points to the pervasive tendency in education research and policy to continue to see schools as closed spaces, existing within set boundaries that neither penetrate into the worlds beyond those borders nor allow those worlds to seep into their perimeters. Finally, I suggest that in the process of allowing youth to develop their own places, spaces of possibility emerge in which young people can interrogate and negotiate social forces acting upon them. It is this final conclusion that perhaps leads to a sense of hope. These three conclusions formed the basis of continued work on youth, spaces, and cities. If one could find these spaces of possibility then it would seem that the political project comes into focus; an educative project formed in the hope of working toward more places where students can "get what they need," get "in the mix," and, perhaps even find family.

Note

1 In my time at the WELL, only the staff mentioned the presence of cameras in the lab. This comment by a student makes me think that the staff point out the surveillance to offending patrons when situations threaten violence but it is not a part of the common lab-goers' mindset.

4

GEOGRAPHIES OF SCHOOL REFORM

The move from Durham, North Carolina to Indianapolis, Indiana took me from the South (albeit known at the time as the "Progressive South") to the Midwest, although I quickly learned that Indiana is sometimes called the "northernmost Southern state." I was never quite sure what that meant, as it was invoked in differing and confusing times. There always seemed to be some kind of a wink and a nod—signaling something about race. To cross these regions, I followed highways streamlining through the Appalachian Mountains, along the length of Tennessee, and then into the bluegrass horse country of Kentucky, turning north abruptly in Louisville. Most of the drive still feels like the South, even Southern Indiana has a lush, slow stillness to it. But then things start to flatten out. Indiana University, where I was headed for my first academic position, has its main campus in Bloomington to the south of Indianapolis, creating a bit of a progressive, multicultural hub just outside where the Ku Klux Klan had a power structure in the 1920s and continues to have a presence today. Doctoral students of color who drove up to Indianapolis often talked of the common understanding that one didn't want to stop for gas between Bloomington and the capital; there were known sundown towns, places where you'd better not be after dark if you were a person of color.

Still, Indianapolis feels more like a Midwestern than a Southern city. Its reputation as "the crossroads of America" means train tracks, expanding highways and beltways, and, at least at one time, significant industrial spaces and facilities. Many of those expanses stood empty as I drove in, some soon to be converted to apartments and multi-use spaces—the changes would come quick. Indianapolis is at the western end of the Rust Belt, a moniker for the fading impact of the automobile industry in the Midwest. Meridian Street bifurcates the city, and it didn't take me long to learn that, historically, blacks were allowed to work east of the landmark street but, again, had better not be there after dark.

The city was and is deeply segregated, with a pronounced urban core and whitening suburbs encircling the city. For me, this segregation felt different than Southern racial dynamics;

it was deeply felt spatial distinction, materially racialized spaces as opposed to different roles within those spaces. The New South tended to be segregated in role or position but not material space. As I adjusted to this new professional context, I sought out community connections with local advocates and activists to try and understand the city, its neighborhoods, its history, and its politics. Before I could start to map those geographies of affect and bodies, I had to know the lay of the land; I had to understand how it had already been mapped and what layers would need to be uncovered to see through multiple scales. Perhaps then I could see what those maps were teaching us.

School Reform in Indianapolis

In order to explain further what taking space seriously in educational inquiry might look like, I turn to my former home and scholarly context for 10 years, the midsized Midwestern city of Indianapolis, Indiana. Continuing to follow Soja's (1989) call for the "reassertion of space in critical social theory," the journey to Indianapolis offers insight into the ways in which everyday lives, everyday bodies, and everyday spaces of schools and schooling are entangled in material, affective, and discursive forces. In the previous two chapters, I showed how these forces affected the WELL, mapping them at the level of school, classroom, and bodies. In this chapter, I explore these forces as they travel under the marker of educational reform, redrawing the maps of districts, communities, and classrooms alike.

To do this, however, necessarily involves critical inquiry into both the hegemonic forces at work and the resistance marshaled in response to the spatial understanding of schools; this approach often reveals hidden mappings of race, class, sexualities, dis/abilities, and gender, and their intersections. Further, these hidden maps can be traced to underlying assumptions and biases loaded into concepts such as community, identity, place, and space. When analyses are overly rooted in the historical without consideration of the spatial, theorization runs the risk of the critique that, "we have forgotten or overlooked the social relationships (primarily relationships of production)" of urban contexts (Lefebvre, 1991, p. 1). Or as Gulson and Symes (2007) suggest, "the failure to entertain the spatial dynamics and exigencies underpinning education, in any full blooded way, will result in understandings of education's context, policy and practice that, at best, will be narrow, and, perhaps, at worst, flawed" (p. 107). Turning the tools of Critical Geography to education reform, my analysis of Indianapolis embodies a hope for new ways to problematize, analyze, and address the contexts in which we work and are worked upon, hidden and otherwise.

The education reform movement nationally found close allies in Indiana's largely Republican leadership with the 2004 election of Governor Mitch Daniels. Moving quickly to capitalize on Democratic support of charter schools in Indianapolis, leaders sought to expand charters in a model outside of traditional public school districts, began work on providing vouchers for private and religious schools, and actively worked to minimize the effectiveness of the teacher's union. Talking points from the conservative American Legislative Exchange Council (ALEC) and advocacy groups such as the Fordham Foundation paved the way for what I came to see as a master class in state political maneuvering. In many ways, Indiana in the mid to late 2000s was "the point of the spear" of the education reform movement.

To analyze the changes this movement wrought in Indianapolis, I follow the model of Lipman's (2011) *New Political Economy of Urban Education: Neoliberalism, Race, and the Right to the City*. In an accessible and comprehensive account of the ways in which Chicago is undergoing this form of remapping, Lipman (following a few others) lays out the basic strategy as "expansion of the central business district, racial containment through slum clearance and construction of public housing, multiple tax authorities to mask fiscal crises, and deflection of African American resistance through cooptation of Black politicians into the city's political machine" (pp. 27–28). She further delineates the process by detailing what she terms "neoliberal restructuring" and lists the following as the major components: marketing the city for investment and consumption, gentrification, a racialized urban imaginary of "blight" and "revitalization," tax increment financing (known as TIFs), the university as real estate developer, and the expanded influence of markets and privatization. Not only does Lipman's work provide a model for my analysis of Indianapolis (although the particularities of place still matter), I also follow her in arguing that the "twin logics of capital accumulation and White supremacy" (p. 148) drive this particular machine. Education reform efforts in Indianapolis mirror this model of neoliberal restructuring and embrace a market logic that is seen as both "commonsense" and inevitable. Like Chicago, the ways in which places matter to folks that interact with them has largely been invisible, ignored, and politically inconvenient.

To better understand these processes spatially, the metaphor of Geographic Information Systems (GIS) is useful. GIS is a process by which spatial data are represented digitally and through which multiple variables can be layered over each other, creating a variegated cartographic representation (i.e., a map). Scholars in education use GIS and collaborate with cartographies in inquiry projects that include educational variables and explore the intersectional nature of other social indicators as a way of better understanding spatial relations and distribution (see Cobb 2020; Yoon & Lubienski, 2018; Helfenbein & Clauser, 2008; Tate, 2008, Taylor, 2007). While I do not literally use GIS technology here, I similarly attempt to understand how multiple layers of data—for example, the hidden maps of racial containment—all come together to represent the complex set of forces at work in the schools and communities in Indianapolis.

This analysis shows how efforts of contemporary education reform effectively remap the city and its relationship to public education. Highlighting maps as a discursive tool, this critical analysis also allows for inquiry into the production of very material effects as schools and communities are labeled as deficient and, by proxy, so too are its citizens, teachers, and students. The defunding of traditional public schools, the rise of charter schools, and private school vouchers in urban contexts serve as both justification for and offer solution to a reconstruction of the neoliberal educational city. Using the framework of Critical Geography, new understandings emerge as we focus on how the deterritorialization/reterritorialization of urban contexts affects the lived experience of schools. This is the spaciocurricular at work.

Hidden Maps of the City

In Indianapolis, the geography of the public schools necessarily begins with a consideration of scale and attendant notions of political economy and impact. Indianapolis Public Schools (IPS) is the urban school district (read: historically black schools). Interestingly, its schools were integrated until 1920 when, with the creation of an all-black high school, segregated education began and the townships developed into suburban nodes—although today they are remarkably and increasingly urban in characteristics—surrounding the traditional urban core. This decentralization of schooling occurred even while most other public services were consolidated under local governance in 1968 (Reynolds, 1998, p. 186).

The historical *placement* of the black community through lending practices, real estate redlining (see Map 2), the development of public housing, and deliberate coercion through the actions of groups like the Ku Klux Klan (1920s–1950s) shifted to active *displacement* through the construction of highway systems (1960–1970), the refusal of redevelopment funds for black communities, and the subsequent construction of the Indiana University Purdue University Indianapolis campus (1969). Indianapolis Deputy Mayor at the time, John Walls, remarked that the expanding university campus and the highway construction were: "a major part of the concern that the black community had regarding housing in the community. They—here as elsewhere—were fearful that renewal meant displacement, which, of course, it did" (quoted in Pierce, 2005, p. 81).

At the time, white flight was rampant in the face of desegregation (as it was across the nation)[1]. The difference in Indianapolis was that white families did not have to go far as the urban planning model of creating townships surrounding the urban core enabled both racial containment and white access to the jobs and services of downtown. Desegregation and white flight can be seen as exemplars of the political characteristics of scale[2] playing out in particular ways in this place. It also should be noted that the same highway system that displaced and dispersed historic black communities also made suburbanization possible— it provided easy infrastructural access between downtown jobs and suburban homes; this can be seen in urban areas across the country (e.g., Los Angeles, Chicago, and Washington, D.C.,). At the same time, gentrification efforts tended to follow the historical model of protecting and isolating certain spaces as racial and socio-economic diversity encroached. Each of these forces—resistance to desegregation, white flight, racialized urban planning, gentrification—played out

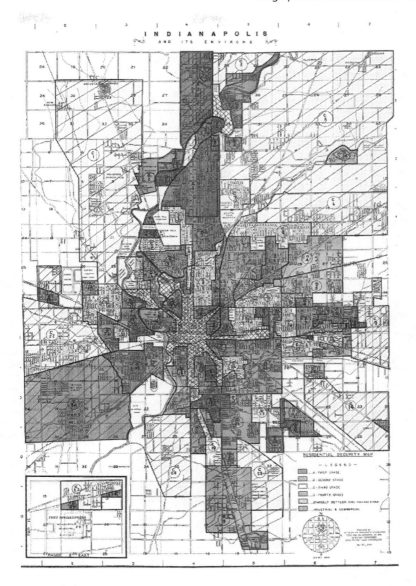

MAP 2 1937 Redline Map: Residential Security Map of Indianapolis, IN (public domain).

in Indianapolis. The hidden map of the city reveals the sedimented racial history of urban development that de/reterritorialized neighborhoods as the desirability of the urban shifted over time. All of these characteristics point to the particularities of place in a spatial analysis: the context within which the lived experiences of school take place.

In Indianapolis, this functioned effectively as racial containment, political disenfranchisement, and economic disinvestment for particular communities. What resulted was clear inequity in terms of educational opportunity and access to jobs and economic advancement that formed the contours of this segregated city. Of course, I am arguing here that these moves were intentional, capitalizing on racial animus that is ever-present but somewhat under the surface in the Midwest. Development too often serves to obscure the racialized containment that results from these policies; white spaces operate as whiteness itself in that they obfuscate its origins, its politics, and the structures that reinforce and maintain its persistence. This hidden map (or what Edward Soja might call 2nd Space) functioned precisely as it was intended, much like Duncan-Andrade's contention that urban education is not failing but rather doing exactly what it was designed to do.

The contemporary conjuncture, however, presents a challenge to the existing mapping. White flight and suburbanization are no longer the priority within the politics of development but are now replaced with interests in the economic potential for the urban core: this newer layer of the map is the more recent trend of downtown gentrification efforts, happening in cities nationwide. Rearticulating this new sense of urbanism requires dismantling the previous representations of urban space as dangerous, undesirable, and largely to be avoided. In short, the rhetoric of failed urban education and its hidden intent of moving residents out to the suburbs was *too* successful and an alternative was now needed to remap urban contexts.

Remapping the Next City

The landscape of education reform in Indianapolis has been dominated by two interconnected groups: The office of the Deputy Mayor for Education (created 2012) and the non-profit Mindtrust (created in 2006). An early charter school authorizer, the Mayor's office of Indianapolis and their charter school board began running its own (i.e., not affiliated with IPS) portfolio of schools in Indianapolis in 2001. The Mindtrust was constructed to support "innovation in education" and to carry on the work of the Democratic Mayor who led the initial charter school reform initiative. The first steps they took were to provide highly competitive grants for educational programs in Indianapolis and an early concern arose with the realization that all of the early winners were from out of state (notably affiliated with Harvard, Columbia, and Stanford). The several community groups that I worked with were quite frustrated that they had applied to something they apparently were not really in the running for. So, similar to Lipman's list of strategies in Chicago, the contemporary education reform movement in Indianapolis seemed to operate along an easily identifiable path: charter school expansion with an attendant state and philanthropic funding set of support structures, increased mayoral role, divestment in local resources in favor of national actors (evidence of a complex national network), and the unapologetic framing of education as economic development for cities.

In spring of 2013, two reports were released to the public regarding plans for restructuring educational opportunities for the city of Indianapolis. The first, *The shared challenge of quality schools: A place-based analysis of school performance in Indianapolis*, represents a coalition of education organizations and promises to identify "where the greatest number of children need better access to high-performing schools in order to enhance the focus of education reform" (p. 3) and divides the city into priority areas based on the Indiana Department of Education A–F grading scale for schools. The second, the *Neighborhoods of Educational Opportunity* plan produced through the Mayor of Indianapolis' office, offers a similar analysis based on what they termed "high-quality seats" that provided a framework to map the city's communities based on student achievement.

These remapped city streets require a cartographic approach to understandings how "all our lived spaces have been shifting from a period of crisis-generated restructuring to the onset of a new era of restructuring-generated crisis, a crisis deeply imbricated in the post-modernization of the contemporary world" (Soja, 1996, p. 23). In this case, the need to make downtown areas desirable again for high-end development restructured how those urban areas were understood by financial capital, developers, and young professionals that might choose to move there from the suburbs. Suddenly, the "crisis" of urban education in Indianapolis required creative, innovative solutions—solutions outside of the traditional public school system—and it didn't hurt that those efforts might be monetized by the private section as well as serve certain ideological concerns. The reterritorialization efforts here follow Lefebvre's conception of the "state

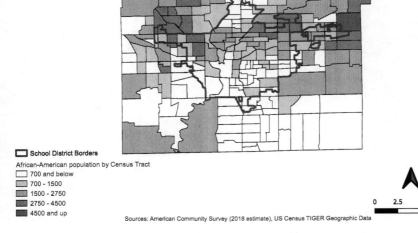

School District Borders

African-American population by Census Tract
700 and below
700 - 1500
1500 - 2750
2750 - 4500
4500 and up

0   2.5   5 mi

Sources: American Community Survey (2018 estimate), US Census TIGER Geographic Data

MAP 3   Racial Demographics of Indianapolis Public Schools: Marion County, IN

mode of production" where public policy at multiple scales is leveraged as part of economic extraction strategy.

The first plan for remapping Indianapolis highlighted not only the creation of so-called "opportunity schools" but also included Mayoral control of the majority African-American and low SES urban school district, switching control of this district from an elected school board to a Mayor appointed school board. The plan was presented with colorful, professional handouts, well-constructed PowerPoints, and in well-attended, high-profile public meetings. Arguing that the urban communities of Indianapolis were unable to vote for and support educational policy that actually benefited their children, the Mindtrust offered that the broader electorate of the Mayor office was better positioned to meet the needs of IPS students. In this way, the plan specifically called for disenfranchisement of certain bounded citizens (i.e., black) with no suggestion that the same was necessary in the white or even more-white surrounding districts; in other words, democratic control was acceptable for some but not all.

As the plan became increasingly public, questions began to arise around the implications for black families and the students that attended IPS schools. The Education Working Group of the local NAACP began a detailed project of critiquing the plan. Striking to me is that I remember thinking the reformers here were legitimately surprised by the backlash which further evidences a deep disconnect with the communities that these so-called reformers claim to want to help. This plan, unveiled with significant PR and flourish, rather quickly faded away—significant too in that it was funded by $750,000 from the Indiana Department of Education then run by now disgraced Superintendent of Public Instruction Tony Bennett.[3] Rarely mentioned in public discussion of the plan, the State of Indiana had funded these efforts and therefore supported what amounted to anti-democratic education reform.

The next move came from the Mayor's office with what was termed the NEO (neighborhoods of educational opportunity) plan—packaged in another slick set of materials and presentations—and, this time, emphasized a broader coalition of organizations including the libertarian Milton Friedman Foundation, a university-based center, Stand for Children, and certain notable leaders of color in the city. Mayoral control was dropped and the emphasis shifted from opportunity schools to zones, priority areas, service gaps, and what they came to call "neighborhood schools." The city was being quite clearly reterritorialized in ways that not only reinforced processes of gentrification but also targeted the next neighborhoods for development, with school reform leading the way.

Part of my point here is both that critique and public response can be effective in not only changing the shape of education reform, but also that the resulting shifts often enfold discursive aspects of the critique while not changing the overall direction. Certainly, initial efforts by the local NAACP and other black leaders in the community successfully pushed back on the most egregious aspects of the new educational map of Indianapolis. But, the resources behind these education reform efforts are substantial and are levied from the city, state, and national scales. It soon became clear that the language employed in these efforts (i.e., opportunity schools and neighborhoods of educational opportunity) was indeed national and would resurface in Chicago, Baltimore, and other urban areas. In short, the reform efforts here were led by smart, adaptable people; these capabilities can also be referred to as hegemonic power. Further, the spatial characteristics of both the plans and the racial dynamics within which they play out clearly matter.

Inequity Remapped

What we then see is how the layered map of education reform begins with a sociohistorical reality rooted in racism and class struggle, material borders and boundaries directly impacting the lives of people in the city. As the changes of a global economic system come into play in Midwestern cities, Indianapolis confronts a need to restructure—to remap. It does this not in response to obvious educational inequity but, rather, to create new spaces for development more appropriate to a changing world of work (i.e., factories become condos, neighborhoods gentrify, and development drives public policy). Schools find themselves in the middle of this mix; disenfranchised and defunded for decades, they now become the problem that only the market can fix. All of this plays out spatially as the city becomes reterritorialized with certain neighborhoods labeled as "opportunity zones" and others become the new, scattered spaces for the displaced poor.

While the spaces being remapped here are without question poor, it cannot be overstated that they are also raced. The covalence of race and poverty in the United States is well documented but, in attempting to understand these new maps, the importance of foregrounding the racial politics undergirding these efforts remains paramount. Worth quoting at length, McKittrick's (2006) groundbreaking book *Demonic Grounds: Black Women and the Cartographies of Struggle* provides an exposition on how this process works across races, bodies, and spaces:

> If prevailing geographic distributions and interactions are racially, sexually and economically hierarchical, these hierarchies are naturalized by repetitively spatializing "difference." That is, 'placing' the world within an ideological order, unevenly. Practices of domination, sustained by a unitary vantage point, naturalize both identity and place, repetitively spatializing where nondominant groups 'naturally' belong. This is, for the most part, accomplished through economic, ideological, social, and political processes that see and position the racial-sexual body within what seem like predetermined, or appropriate, places and assume that this arrangement is commonsensical.
>
> (p. xv)

Expanding on Massey's (1995) work that highlights how the "inevitability" of spatial arrangements undergirds late capitalism, McKittrick points to how difference—race, gender, and their intersections—is spatialized and how those socio-material arrangements are reinforced and perpetuated through their naturalization. For our purposes, we see how the education reform movement in Indianapolis remapped the city to serve the interests of development and obscure the impact of such moves on the racialized bodies affected. Importantly, I draw attention to the maps—hidden and otherwise—whose categories and zones are defined by accountability systems, which reduce schools to a metric of "quality seats," and whose logic seems to be that fixing education will fix poverty. There are no people in these reform maps, there is no history, but the spaciocurricular lessons are clear. I'm reminded of a meeting with the Deputy Mayor of Education that I attended with folks from the education group of the NAACP, at which one person commented: "this is a lovely economic plan you have here. When can we talk about the education of our children?"

I end this part of the journey with the hope of Lawrence Grossberg (again noting that Critical Geography has close ties to cultural studies via Birmingham), offering it as one that might be shared by critical scholars in the field of education as well. The hope is that this type of historical spatial analysis will "contribute to the conversation through which we might find again the possibility of imagining alternative futures, and through which we might choose a less destructive direction for the undiscovered possibilities of kids' present and future lives" (Grossberg, 2005, p. 12). The undiscovered possibilities for children are precisely what is at stake in our ongoing struggles over the role of education in civil society—precisely why education theorists should write back. I remind the reader of the earlier discussion of "spaces of possibility" as learned at the WELL and suggest that educational researchers might find these spaces with young people that are—in ways clear and sometimes not—carving them out for themselves. Not only does critical geography and the spaciocurricular offer new possibilities for scholarship in curriculum theory to do this work, but this approach is particularly necessary because spatial tools are already in play in contemporary education reform. The city is, yet again, being remapped, and our political project begins in understanding those processes in the effort to organize, respond, and resist.

Notes

1 In 1979, the US District Court found Indianapolis Public Schools guilty of racial segregation and busing policies began in 1981.
2 I remind the readers of the discussion of deterritorialization and reterritorialization in Chapter 1; see also Helfenbein & Buendia (2017).
3 In 2013, Tony Bennett resigned as the Education Commissioner for the State of Florida amid allegations that his office gamed Indiana's school rating system to benefit a charter school run by a GOP benefactor.

5

THE GLOBAL CITY

Taking Space Seriously

Starting in 2006, my intellectual geography expanded as I began to do international work around geography and democratic education. Beginning in the lovely country of Macedonia and culminating in a sabbatical that included Kenya, Malawi, and South Africa, I began to consider cities around the world and the ways in which youth and schooling played a role in constructing those landscapes; conversely, I looked for the ways in which those landscapes, both affective and material, impacted schooling and youth. These were long trips, weary travel that paid back beautiful vistas, new tastes and smells, and close interaction with people and cultures whose surface I merely scratched. The work in Macedonia revolved around moving beyond the pain of the recent Balkan conflicts and a desire for the new promises of the European Union. The African context too sought to distance itself from both the colonial and postcolonial authoritarian mode and turned its eye to global capitalism. All that I interacted with seemed highly concerned with global relations—seen as both positive and negative—and the ghosts of colonization, apartheid, and dictatorship were everywhere; haunted landscapes these.

Universities have long been interested in connecting with international partners and attracting students from abroad. In the last twenty years or so however, higher education came to see these international connections as new revenue streams that were increasingly important as state and federal funding was increasingly cut. Some campuses were ahead of the game and had steady relationships on which to build on, while others added these goals to strategic plans and mission statements without much concern for the necessary interpersonal work that success often required. Of course, as anyone who has traveled knows, being from the United States abroad is fraught with both love and hate. For me, building trust and meaningful relationships serve as the beginning point to any of these efforts but this was not easy as trust was only cautiously given and often hard to come by. Seeing globalization and universities efforts at internationalization from another vantage point brought some things into focus and it's worth remembering that internationalization is by definition a curriculum project. How the global city has developed internationally and what the curriculum of our efforts to work with those sites comes to be are the questions taken up here.

In beginning to consider the global city, I am reminded of the common effect while traveling—that of feeling of being out of place. This feeling is not just geographic as a scholar from the United States in cities such as Skopje, Cape Town, Lilongwe, and New Delhi but also in the sense that one joins a conversation that is already underway and, further, in the sense that my work comes from a particular branch of curriculum theorizing (what we refer to as the Reconceptualization) that may or may not immediately resonate with those already engaged in international work. In addition, my work does not focus on comparative education specifically but rather takes youth in the globalized city as its object of analysis, in and of both formal and informal educative spaces. I do not however see this as necessarily a bad thing; in fact, I have argued that there are potentially productive possibilities in being "out of place" and that there are dangers in attending too closely with staying within one's comfortable borders, or, as is commonly said, knowing one's place.

According to Childress (2010) four rationales for curriculum internationalization provide a framework for understanding not only motivation for internationalization work but perhaps some insight into a deeper analysis of means and ends. Following the 1999 OECD report on Quality and Internationalization in Higher Education, academic, economic, political, and socio-cultural rationales seem to characterize the field. In my own experience within the US context (and confirmed by Childress) the economic and political seem to dominate the discussion. One could argue that the academic and socio-cultural could also be thought of as ethical rationales particularly if one places the conversation on internationalization within a much larger debate on the role of the university and education itself. In this way, I want to acknowledge that ethical concerns and tensions form a foundation on which my approach is built. Key to these tensions remains acknowledging that curriculum—both higher education and pre-university—has traditionally been rooted in national culture (Pinar 2003; 2006) and that the easiest way for an institution to take up questions of internationalization would be to frame them within economic and political interests. My hope however lies in the possibility of pushing back to some degree by privileging an ethical approach to curriculum work. To take on the charge leveed by Miller (2005): "we must work our relationships to one another if we are to construct and reconstruct the curriculum field as an ongoing and human project, incapable of closure yet dedicated to talking action in order to create 'what should be and what might be'" (p. 213).

Geography, Curriculum, and Globalization

Globalization, and the newer term internationalization, continues to be discussed in higher education policy, strategic planning, and educational research settings, and in many ways is increasingly taken as a given "state of things" that precludes careful examination. Attendant terms such as neoliberalism and neoconservatism have also been bandied about in conversations and presentations at professional meetings and in scholarly publication. However, the implications—and for that matter, contested nature of all these terms—rarely seems to enter into the leadership or discourse or often, the analysis. For those interested in social education and critical educational projects writ large; this lacuna holds significant potential for inquiry.

The border and the way in which it means differently within globalized sets of spatial relations becomes an important object of analysis in critical geographies; indeed, these entanglements of borders and global/local contexts can come to be seen as fundamental concerns in a discussion of curriculum internationalization. While much has been made of the "spatial turn" in social theorizing, it remains important to note yet again that Critical Geography insists on the addition of spatial analysis beyond the merely discursive. While valuing and acknowledging the important work in recognizing the ways in which language helps to construct spaces, a Critical Geography seeks to then take the oft-neglected next step of analyzing how those spaces *materially* change, change over time, and impact the lived, embodied world. Seeing spaces as relational—a geography of the entangled nature of space, place, power, and identity emerges to point to new understandings of people in the world. My work in Macedonia considered complex set of relations in striking ways as teachers and curricularists there took up the task of education reform in their hopes of future acceptance into the European Union. Internationalization for them was not a choice but rather a political strategy in the hopes of having some say in continuing conflict over national identity, regional redefinition, and the economic promises of a global marketplace. In fact, globalization itself and its impact on a newly reconstituted country was a concept of significate debate and my curriculum work there became a project of facilitating a process with the educators there revolving around three questions borrowed from the US Civil Rights Movement: (1) what parts of the dominant culture do you want?, (2) what parts of the dominant culture do you not want?, and (3) what parts of your own culture do you want to keep? One can see that this focus on the tension between the local and global is wrapped around an ethical axis—one that holds both commitments that international curriculum work is fundamentally an engagement with the other and that such interactions exist within very real power relations (i.e., the recognition of dominance). This is further explored in the chapter of the edited book 2012 *Ethics and International Curriculum Work: The Challenges of Culture and Context* entitled "A new set of questions: The ethics of taking space seriously in Macedonia" (Helfenbein, 2012).

Internationalization of the Curriculum

The terms "globalization" and "internationalization" are often used in discussion of the transformations of economic, political, and cultural structures in the contemporary moment. Defenders of an economic globalization (e.g., Friedman,

1999) see hope in the neoliberal ideas that the "free market" itself will normalize and equalize social relations through its guaranteed influence; essentially, so the argument goes, the principles and responses of the market plays the role that ethics might have otherwise. Of course, other theorists suggest that we might merely characterize these forces as operating a centerless hegemony, as empire instead of imperialism (Hardt & Negri, 2000; 2004). Important in my analysis here lies the recognition that the new sets of spatial relations offered are to be interrogated intentionally on intersectional, ethical grounds. I hope by now it is clear that I prefer the latter. Although the scale of such thinking may be daunting, feminist urban geographer Leslie Kern reminds us that "scale and complexity aren't excuses for throwing our hands up in the face of a problem. What is clear is that whatever interventions we produce have to take into account the spatial and the social, public and private, and above all, they must be intersectional" (2020, pp. 160–161).

These vague and frankly monolithic conceptions of globalization and internationalization are not simply the result of lazy thinking (at least not entirely). Doreen Massey (2005) notes that the political rhetoric of globalization revolves around its inevitability, and, as a consequence, casts the nations and regions of the world that evidence difference in economic structure as "behind." Without question, persistent rhetoric surrounding global economic crises and the subsequent bailouts follows a logic of inevitability: that is, this had to be done. But, interestingly, it had to be done *because* of the interconnected nature of global markets and supply chains. This "sleight of hand" functions by turning "geography into history, space into time" (Massey, 2005, p. 5). Obviously, as a geographer—indeed a founder of Critical Geography and feminist geographies within Cultural Studies—this is of concern for her, but the point is a larger one. Massey asks what is at stake in the occluding of geographic difference within a logic of global inevitability? What is at stake for educators in Macedonia? Malawi? South Africa? India? What might be generative in having educators answer the question of "what is internationalization?" for themselves—what is _____ (insert country name here) in a set of contemporary global relations and what is at stake in those answers? What if we challenged the logic of inevitability?

The study of societies, schooling, and youth informed by a critical spatial analysis privileges an acknowledgement of the complex geographies of everyday life within an always already globalized space. To open this trajectory for analysis up, one begins with a theoretical positioning of schooling—in the same way as Lefebvre's city—as a "possibilities machine" (Soja, 1996, p. 81) where "to change life we must change space" (Lefebvre, 1991, p. 190) and indeed this process is always, already at work whether we acknowledge it or not. Critical social theory afforded us a language aimed at encapsulating what it meant to be strictured by and committed to ideological contexts, as well as repressed by institutional apparatuses. It was also this trajectory of theorizing that opened up space, made it a mandate for cultural workers to grasp a cultural context where discursive practices defined material conditions and the multiplicity of experience. To a large degree the potential of seeing space in this way, as a conduit to changing the conditions of engagement, remains largely unrecognized in educational theorizing; but, now, when identity, assemblage, and experience are increasingly laid open by shifting socio-economic and technological forces the need for educators to creatively engage in social practices and take space seriously seems all the more essential.

An example of how theory might inform such projects has been the conceptualization of what J.K. Gibson-Graham calls an "ethics of the local." Gibson-Graham (2003) has informed my own engagement in thinking through what the global city is, represents, and offers as potentiality. This "ethics of the local" as an integral component of any examination of globalization and its material effects provides a constructive way of interrogating notions of the global. Gibson-Graham contends:

> Globalization discourse situates the local (and thus all of us) in a place of subordination, as "the other within" of the global order. At worst it makes victims of localities and robs them of economic agency and self-determination. Yet in doing so globalization suggests its own antidote, particularly with respect to the economy: imagine what it would mean, and how unsettling it would be to all that is now in place, if the locality were to become the active subject of its economic experience.
>
> (p. 3)

This is to say that too often in social theory, the complex and contradictory conditions of global capitalism are reduced and simplified into terms that are not only hollowed out of meaning but potentially dangerous in the ways that they obscure their exceptions as well as their lived, embodied impacts on both people and the material world. Much like the insistence of cultural studies scholars that *culture* be seen as a process instead of a *thing*, the usage of the term globalization—or global capitalism for that matter—benefits from an understanding of its fluidity, its changing, adaptive behavior in a world where we make our own history under conditions not of our own making. Highlighting the way globalization processes move through the processes of deterritorialization, reterritorialization, and mapping, forces of globalization can be seen as pulsing extensions of the often-contradictory processes of capital throughout the spatial realm. What Lefebvre calls the "incessant to-and-fro" describes how the pursuit of new markets to exploit, the reinscription of old markets to new ends, and the construction of markets where there once were none clearly becomes an analytic explicitly important as we consider the commodification of public education. Lefebvre (2003) argues that these processes follow the broadly conceived characteristics of urbanization. As these processes extend through the spatial, we see—sometimes slowly, sometimes quickly—the urbanization of everything (Helfenbein, 2011a). Following Lefebvre, global capital follows this trajectory in spaces that would not necessarily have to be considered global cities *per se*. Rather, when these urbanities are seen as sets of relations they become pervasive and attempting to find spaces outside of those relations becomes increasingly difficult. In a similar way, Said (1993) offers that, "Just as none of us is outside or beyond geography, none of us is completely free from the struggle over geography. That struggle is complex and interesting because it is not only about soldiers and cannons but also about ideas, about forms, about images and imaginings" (p. 6).

However, what is compelling argued by Sassen (2014) is that we are increasingly seeing people and places expelled from access to economic systems as a result of new "predatory formations" within late capitalism. This expulsion results from the convergence of economic elites and systemic structures—all originating in the urban centers of power—that enable them to determine who is "in" and who is "out" (see also Tsing, 2005). Striking in my international work was how evident these processes are. Whether it was ethnic strife in Macedonia or the plight of African youth who find themselves without economic possibility even though they played the neoliberal game in terms of education and participation. It wasn't the commodification of youth that was most visible but, rather, their expulsion from the economic milieu. What then is at hand is indeed an urban revolution—not only in terms of the intensity in which material experience is impacted by the convergence of global forces but also in the necessity for new analytics to make those dynamics visible.

Helpful in similar ways, Anna Tsing's detailed ethnographies refuse the tendency to obscure the relations between agency and structure by notably highlighting the friction between global and local forces. She states,

> The challenge here is to move from situated, that is "local," controversies to widely circulating or "global" issues of power and knowledge and back, as this allows us to develop understandings of the institutions and dialogues in which both local and global cultural agendas are shaped.
>
> (Tsing, 1994, p. 279)

Similar to a previous call of "thinking through scale" (Helfenbein 2011b), what's called for here is a method and analytic process that is attendant to forces and agencies in relation rather than distinct, universalizing, or determined. This approach reveals the inherent flaws in both the system and our understandings of it, implying a critique of big data analytics, their impact on internationalization, and the dangers in their assumptions. Here lie the ruins.

> Even as technologies of scalability advance, the charm of world-making scalability is unraveling in our times. Scalability spreads—and yet it is constantly abandoned, leaving ruins. We need a nonscalability theory that pays attention to the mounting pile of ruins that scalability leaves behind."
>
> (Tsing, 2012, p. 506)

Scalability for Tsing, refers to not only the incessant desire with global capital to "go to scale" but, importantly, also a critique of an insistence within social theory that our explanatory frameworks are global in nature, serving to obscure what's left behind. She continues,

> Nonscalability theory requires attention to historical contingency, unexpected conjuncture, and the ways that contact across difference can produce new agendas. In earlier work, I have called these processes 'friction.' …If the world is still diverse and dynamic, it is because scalability never fulfills its own promises.
>
> (p. 510)

The point here being that "if the world is still diverse and dynamic" (and it is, as evidenced by a mushroom at the end of the world) we necessarily turn to new analytics that highlight the ways in which we see, understand, and perhaps politically make more possible those agendas.

Tsing's attention to the margins shines light on how these interactions are lived, resisted, and negotiated—over and over again—highlighting uncertainty or perhaps, the awkwardness, necessary in an analysis. But this too is a careful and nuanced understanding of margins that sees potential and possibility:

> Nor do I refer to margins as the sites of deviance from social norms. Instead, I use the term to indicate an analytic placement that makes evident both the constraining, oppressive quality of cultural exclusion and the creative potential of rearticulating, enlivening, and rearranging the very social categories that peripheralize a group's existence. … My interest is in the zones of unpredictability at the edges of discursive stability, where contradictory discourses overlap, or where discrepant kinds of meaning-making converge; these are what I call margins.
>
> (1994, p. 279)

Here we see another type of friction—that of an analysis that insists on focusing on both the constraints and creative potential as work in the processes of making meaning in the world. Not contradiction but negotiation; the friction here is where the action is.

Rejecting the term culture as too loaded, Tsing suggests that a turn to assemblage may be more productive. Weheliye (2014) states that "assemblages are inherently productive, entering into polyvalent becomings to produce and give expression to previously nonexistent realities, thoughts, bodies, affects, spaces, actions, ideas, and so on" (p.46).As part of Tsing's understanding a particular mushroom and the struggles of agricultural science to fully see its nested relation with global capitalism, she describes "science as translation machine" (p. 217). Translation here points to the messiness and uncertainty—or said another way, a type of epistemic violence—involved in every act of translation. Not only the impossibility of the task but the ways in which our knowledge systems cut and paste aspects of understandings onto/into existing frames serve to create the machine. However, she notes that "layered, inconsistent, and jumbled ontologies form even within the domain of the machine" (p. 218). Therefore,

> The concept of assemblage—an open-ended entanglement of ways of being—is more useful. In an assemblage, varied trajectories gain a hold on each other, but indeterminacy matters. To learn about an assemblage, one unravels its knots.
>
> (Tsing, 2015, p. 83)

This new theorizing of global capitalism then—in its attempt to unravel its knots—turns to the margins, the ruins of a logic and lived experience of capitalism. In doing so, we come to the realization that "civilization and progress turn out to be cover-ups and translation mechanisms for getting access to value procured through violence: classic salvage" (Tsing, 2015, p. 62; see also Wozolek, 2021)[1].

Therefore, thinking with such conceptions as these encourages curricularists to intentionally facilitate new curriculum theories, new modes of inquiry, and new pedagogies or, as Soja would say, new possibilities machines. The space of globalization (or for our purposes here, internationalization and the global city) needs to be seen as a set of forces at work, not guaranteed, and in peoples' relation to it there is possibility: possibility for resistance, possibility for rearticulation, and possibility for an educative project that takes both ethics and assemblage seriously. This spaciocurricular approach of course would work against any logic of inevitability, any "sleight of hand," and push the conversation into one of *what should and might be* within these spaces.

Reconciling Civic Spaces

So then, what is suggested here is that the project of internationalization of the curriculum might find useful the parallel project of curriculum theorizing in addition to curriculum work more traditionally understood—taking space seriously would be one way to take that up. Pinar (2006, p. 163) further suggests that if a goal is one of intellectual advancement in the internationalization of curriculum studies we could adopt "a more sophisticated, self-conscious, judicious participation" in the hopes of staving off what is seen in countries where I've worked (Macedonia, Malawi, South Africa, India) as at meager best standardization and at worst, a new educative hegemony. To that end he offers an approach that takes up both deep projects in the intellectual history of curriculum work in particular places—what he calls verticality—and a return to theory that contextualizes and puts in relation the curriculum projects across/within global spaces—what he terms horizontality (see Pinar 2006, pp. 165–166; Pinar 2003). As institutions continue to negotiate what it might mean to truly and ethically internationalize, the impact on faculty is also significant. Although speaking here about pre-university education, the connections to university faculty seem prescient. Luke (2006) offers that what we seek should be:

> [a] teacher with the capacity to shunt between the local and the global ... a new community of teachers that could and would work, communicate, and exchange—physically and virtually—across national and regional boundaries with each other, with educational researchers, teacher educators, curriculum developers, and, indeed, senior educational bureaucrats.
>
> (p. 135)

The educator in this characterization embraces a fundamentally critical geography approach, understanding the entanglement of space and place within relations of global economic, social, cultural, and affective forces. This type of intersectional educator also understands the importance of recognizing difference with/in place in the effort of making meaning in the world and sharing that approach with their students. This would be a curriculum of taking space seriously.

Luke (2006) continues, "What is needed is a teacher whose very stock [in] trade is to deal educationally with cultural 'others,' with the kinds of transnational and local diversity that is now a matter of course" (Luke, 2006, p. 135). This type of curriculum internationalization would both point us to the intersections of space, place, power, and identity/assemblage and enable new strategies to handle the increasing complexity that defines notions of diversity within a globalized, multi-cultural world. I agree with Luke, who "want[s] to argue for a vision of teaching as cosmopolitan work and a profession in critical and contingent relation to the flows, contexts, and consequences of cultural and economic globalization." (p. 124)

Conclusions/Connections

Working internationally provided insight into global sets of relations that were difficult to see standing only in a US context. While critical geography offers many new possibilities for curriculum work, this chapter suggests that some of the most important works reside in rethinking the role of the civic, an ethics of the local, global, and their relation, and perhaps even the university itself in an increasingly globalized world. I have suggested that "taking space seriously" involves challenging determined, basic conceptions of space and place and putting them into interaction with larger, complex forces of power and identity/assemblage (see Helfenbein 2012). Helping students both K12 and in higher education come into their own as engaged citizens and co-constructors of just and equitable communities requires thoughtful interrogation of commonly taken for granted concepts in our educational institutions. It requires an ethics of the local that rejects efforts at obscuring the forces at work, notably as those forces employ means "favoured in the era of neoliberal urbanism, such as heightened state and corporate surveillance, militarized policing, and the privatization of public space" (Kern, 2020, p. 171). Exploring the global city within an intersectional spatial analysis involves reveling in its entanglements as well as unraveling its knots. In the spirit of Gough (2004), the hope here is for "democratic, multicultural, and transnational citizenries" (p. 4) that might provide for us fresh conceptions of what institutions, spaces and places, and curricula can, might, and perhaps should look like.

Note

1 The author wishes to thank Dr. Gabriel Huddleston for thinking through the work of Tsing in relation to cultural studies and curriculum theorizing.

6

THE CITY AS CURRICULUM

The Baltimore Uprising and Spaces of Exception

After ten years in the Heartland, I was recruited to go to Baltimore and work with a school of education that wanted more community engagement and a much more explicit focus on urban education. This was a move back to the East Coast, not quite the South in my view but close as we were below the Mason-Dixon line. Here too, folks referred to the northern-most Southern city and yet again, I didn't quite know what they meant. There are formal, bordered regions and there are perceptual regions; the later has always seemed more mean-ingful to me. Driving into Baltimore, one is struck by the remnants of industrialization, empty factory spaces and rowhouses clearly built to house their workers. I came to learn that much of the empty rowhouses and storefronts on the Westside could be traced back to the unrest of 1968 and the failure of the city to rebuild, reinvest, or even recognize. Driving toward the Inner Harbor, one can quickly see where the city spends its money. Sports stadi-ums and tourist attractions line the bay with new condo and hotel development spreading east marks quick and clear contrast.

Hard-edged but with character, Baltimore is a city that has a distinct feel, a personality. The first question asked by many Baltimoreans is "where'd you go to high school" which serves as a geographic marker and a source of deep community pride. Located on highway 95 between New York City and Washington DC, with Philadelphian short train ride away, the city benefits from folk coming through: artists, musicians, activists, scholars. But it also has a deep political history that is rooted in a radical, black intellectual tradition. This is where Baltimore felt different from Raleigh or Indianapolis; not that those traditions didn't exist but rather that they were easy to spot, foregrounded in activist circles. I found myself in artist spaces, radical spaces, activist and advocate spaces, and spaces that wove together all those things. I found many powerful, inspirational community leaders who cared deeply about their neighborhoods and the generations of folks that still called them home.

April of 2015 brought national attention to the city of Baltimore as, depend-ing on one's perspective, a *riot* or an *uprising* broke out in response to the death of Freddie Gray at the hands of police. Joining the tragic string of racial violence against black lives by law enforcement—caught on tape and distributed widely via social and traditional media—the events in Baltimore exposed nationally what residents of the city have long known, felt, and lived. Again drawing on the work of Critical Geography, this chapter argues that in pursuit of a deeper contextualization of the Baltimore Uprising (this term is intentional) an examination of the spatialization of the urban context reveals both neoliberal efforts to remap the city and *spaces of exception* within the larger raced and spaced project. The process of redefining/restructuring—a distinction between urbanization as a process and urban as lived experience—then calls into question notions of equity and social justice—particularly in seeing the urban as a part of broader moves that encompass the whole of the social fabric. Expanding out from the larger field of geography, questions have arisen in thinking through what a concept of "spatial justice" (Soja, 2010; Waitoller & Annamma, 2017) might mean and efforts at rethinking citizenship within global sets of forces gives rise to considering differing notions of democracy and identity and event the resurgence of cosmopolitanism as an ethical framework. In thinking in terms of globalization and its impact on the urban, we are reminded that "the social spaces of contemporary capitalism are being increasingly politicized; space is no longer merely the theatre of political conflict but its principle stake" (Brenner, 1997, p. 152). But we are reminded as well that "too often cities have been used only as backdrops and framework in studies of racial and ethnic minorities rather than as an interacting element" (Bayor, 1996, p. xiv). The focus on contemporary Baltimore not also allows for a look analytically at what Lefebvre (2003/1970) calls the "urban problematic" but also frames *the city as curriculum* or, rather, pushes us to ask what these spaces try to teach us?

Connecting all the way back to my dissertation study of the WELL, I have contended that "spaces speak, spaces leak, and spaces of possibility" (Helfenbein 2011a; see Chapters 2 and 3 of this volume) are three heuristics for a spaciocurricular theorizing via Critical Geography. In that work and the work that followed, the spaces of possibility tended to portray possibility as positive (i.e., spaces for resistance and resilience). However, the Baltimore Uprising—while still holding a hopeful possibility as a growing movement continues—highlights the negative counterpart to the concept of spaces of possibility, the space of exception. Specifically, attending to the spatial epicenter of the Uprising, the neighborhood of Sandtown-Winchester, provides insight into spaces beyond marginalization in the sense that certain urban areas (and therefore the lives there) are literally outside the bounds of neoliberal restructuring and the identity forms neoliberalism both needs and creates.

A Bit of Context

The history of Baltimore begins with the port and the deep inland Chesapeake Bay, providing the city with a long history as a hub for trade and with a rather unique borderland identity lying between the cultural North and South.

Incidentally, *Is Baltimore a Southern city today?* remains an interesting question for me. But of importance for our purposes here is the industrial boom coming with the advent of World War II. Following the national trend, port cities and industrial centers in the United States saw massive growth during the war years and the economic prosperity that followed with Baltimore enjoying both. Part of this growth includes what sociologists refer to as the Great Diaspora, referring to the movement of blacks and poor whites from a still predominantly agrarian South into urban areas. While exact numbers are tricky (Alexander *et al.*, 2014) as Baltimore was considered a Southern city, it is estimated that 160,000 workers moved from nearby Southern states between 1940 and 1943. The overall population grew from 859,000 in 1940 to close to 1.3 million in 1943 and, as a marker of this massive change, Baltimore's Bethlehem Steel grew to being the largest steel mill in the country employing over 35,000 people at its peak (Crenson, 2017). However, the city's southern-ness was evidenced as differences between New York City and Philadelphia primarily around the prevalence of Jim Crow and racial segregation. In fact, the first racial residential zoning ordinance in the United States was passed in Baltimore in 1910—this literally and legally made efforts at desegregation illegal (note: it has been commented that while redlining as a practice was created at the University of Chicago, it was first put into practice in Baltimore). An important point to return to later is that this was deemed necessary as the city had long been attractive to free blacks and their growing social and intellectual capital was seen a threat—for good reason. To the point here however, is that regardless of the economic growth in the city post WWII, what is immediately evident is that movement into the middle class was thoroughly raced, and this process was bolstered by what Critical Geographers would call

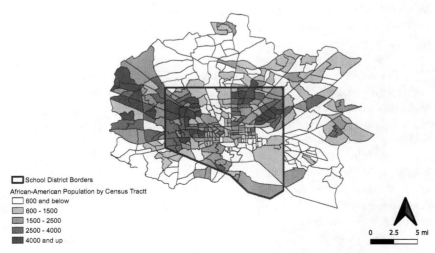

School District Borders
African-American Population by Census Tractt
☐ 600 and below
600 - 1500
1500 - 2500
2500 - 4000
4000 and up

0   2.5   5 mi

Sources: American Community Survey (2018 estimate), US Census TIGER Geographic Data

MAP 4 Racial Demographics of Baltimore Public Schools and Surroundings.

uneven spatial development (Massey, 1978). Takeaway point here: while technically precedent of neoliberal spatio-economic policy and practice, structural racism at the conjuncture of culture and politics set the stage for how things would
play out in Baltimore.

Sandtown-Winchester

All of that post WWII economic growth—while uneven, still growth—eventually went away. By 1990, 75% of jobs in manufacturing, steel production, ship-
building, and transportation were gone and population dropped by 200,000.
Why did the nation's sixth largest city in 1950 fall to twenty-first in 2010. To turn
to the neighborhood home of Freddie Gray and focal point of the Baltimore
Uprising, Sandtown-Winchester differs greatly from many neighborhoods in
the city as well as the city as a whole (although, it should be noted that there
are several neighborhoods not currently getting attention that are in fact quite
similar). Once known as "Baltimore's Harlem," a vibrant black cultural and intellectual space, the neighborhood never recovered from the unrest of 1968 following the assassination of Martin Luther King. Today, the median household
income of Sandtown-Winchester/Harlem Park is $23,000 a year, less than 60%
of Baltimore City as a whole. Unemployment rate is 21%, almost double that of
the city while the neighborhood's poverty rate (approximately 31%) is double
that of the city and one-third of the homes in the neighborhood are aban-
doned—four times the vacant building density of the city. Housing as it is in the
neighborhood has a lead paint violation rate over three times the city's (39.8 vs.
11.8). Baltimore residents represent over 1/3 of Maryland's incarcerated population and Sandtown-Winchester/Harlem Park sends more of its residents to
Maryland prisons than any other Baltimore neighborhood. The area is one of
only five Baltimore neighborhoods to spend $10 million or more on incarcera-
tion. Life expectancy in Sandtown-Winchester/Harlem Park sits at 65.1 years as
opposed to 71.8 in the city as a whole.[1]

In terms of educational attainment, only 6% of the neighborhood's residents
have 4-year college degrees (or more), and over 75% of its residents have either a
high school degree or less. With white flight and the presence of a long-standing
system of private schools, Baltimore City Schools are defined as hypersegregated
with 79.3% of students attending a school of 90% or more minority enrollment
and 44.3% in what has come to be known via the Civil Rights Project as apartheid schools with 99–100% African-American enrollment (Ayscue et al., 2013;
see also Brown, 2015). So, what's happening now in Baltimore is the focused
development of the area known as the Inner Harbor. This is where Camden Yards
and the Ravens stadiums are as well as a large conference center, the "new economy" businesses (primarily tech and finance) and, of course new elegant condos
and renovated industrial spaces converted into apartments—all, by the way with

tax incentives from the city. As Brown (2021) states, "Because of America's spatial racism, White neighborhoods and spaces are imagined as thriving and superior while Black neighborhoods and spaces are deemed as doomed and inferior" (p.4). So, as Levine (1987) notes,

> Baltimore had become "two cities—a city of developers, suburban professionals, and 'back-to-the-city' gentry…and a city of impoverished blacks and displaced manufacturing workers, who continue to suffer from shrinking economic opportunities, declining public services, and neighborhood distress.
>
> (Levine, 1987, p. 103)

The argument here includes two aspects for some interrogation. First, this book as a whole argues that part of what is needed is a scalar geography in analyses of urban spaces within our current moment of globalization. Summer (2019) characterizes these complexities by noting:

> urban planners often imagine the urban environment as spaces to clear (urban renewal), places to fear (racial and spatial profiling, and places to manage (redlining) until they are constructed as desirable spaces again (gentrification).
>
> (p. 175)

The reconsideration of the concept of scale that I propose and a sliding in and out of scales of analysis allows for the recognition of these relations, how they shift over time, and their impacts. Gershon (2017) suggests that this is "an understanding that relationships between micro and macro interactions can be conceptualized as concentric circles from the local to the global and back again. These layers and meanings are nested and emergent and their boundaries are both fluid and porous" (Gershon, 2017, pp. 24–25). This approach to the concept of scale begins with three propositions:

> (1) there is no ontological given to scalar concepts as it is a human heuristic used to describe phenomena; (2) the stakes of the use of these heuristics have experiential and material impact on people—in other words, scale matters; and (3) these heuristics, as they are socially constructed, are complex, contested, and open to change over time.
>
> (Helfenbein & Buendia, 2017, p. 32)

My usage of this approach (as I reflect on it now) typically starts at a tight localized scale—typically kids or classrooms or other educative spaces—and opens, much like the aperture of a camera—to a broader analysis of policy or globalized conditions. What I want to suggest is that this be reversed in the hopes of not losing an emphasis on what for me holds an ethical imperative, to not lose Freddie Gray, a black body, a black body no longer living.

The second move here more directly critiques my own work in the context of trying make some kind of sense of all this. So, I argued in the 2011 collection on post-Reconceptualization what would be a framework for doing critical geographies of education and stated three starting points,

> (1) the subjectivity of our relationship to spaces or...*how spaces speak*; and (2) the lack of guarantee, or determinism, in the nature of both social and spatial production, or *how spaces leak*. Many taking up these two distinctions and their subsequent objects of analysis (e.g., power, identity, positionality, the border, and perhaps most importantly, a rethinking of the global and the local) have come to call their work critical geography, and (3) also point to agency, *the spaces of possibility*.
>
> (p. 314)

Interestingly, over the course of my work to this point in the journey, I have found myself defending the idea that spaces of possibility are indeed agentic, hopeful even, where we find resistance and resilience. I called this my "pathology of hope" in a very early *JCT* piece. But here, in Baltimore, a new stop in the intellectual geography of my work, a new realization came to the fore. I think the Baltimore Uprising and my beginning connections with the activist community in my home there had me thinking that spaces of possibility are not necessarily good. Perhaps this seems obvious but it just hadn't been what I was looking for. Rather, I suggest that the neighborhood of Sandtown/Winchester is a space of exception. When we talk about neoliberalism, we tend to talk about its totalizing nature: there is no outside, there is no alternative. But, increasingly I find this less than convincing or analytically satisfactory; in other words, I'm dubious. Agamben (2005) talks about "the state of exception" in his formulation of sovereignty as going back to the notion of the monarch whose power derives from being not only the source of law of but the exception to it.

As we consider that, "cities, as a rule, do not shrink gracefully" (Alexander *et al.*, 2014, p.29), critical geography opens up considerations of scale and the role of the state in defining spaces and spatial relations—perhaps brought into starkest relief in times of decline. This defining work can be seen as spaciocurricular in that the state operates both materially and pedagogically; as consent is a component of modern political power (in one degree or another), the political is pedagogical. Lefebvre argues that the state cannot be separated from capitalist growth in that the modern state plays a key role in the maintenance and management of global capitalist expansion (Brenner & Elden, 2009, p. 17). His notion of the "state mode of production" offers an alternative to thinking of global capitalism as outside of the nation–state structure and instead suggests that this development traces across "fascism, Stalinism, and Western liberal-democratic models such as the U.S. New Deal and European social democracy" (p. 17). As in our usage of the term scalar in an analysis informed by critical geography, Lefebvre's conception presents "a basis for recognizing the simultaneous extension, differentiation, and fragmentation of social relations across the entire earth under contemporary capitalism" and, most importantly for our purposes here, "the tangled, constantly changing articulation among different scales, from the local, regional, and the national to the worldwide and the planetary and their associated social, political, and economic relations" (p. 23). This again suggests a tension between theoretical perspectives highlighting the structural and those focusing on agency. Process, relation, and interaction mark what geographers refer to as operational scale with bounding the object of analysis considered as cartographic scale. Like other geographic concepts presented in this volume, scale too is expanded beyond an immutable givenness (i.e., a city is a city and a place is a place). This broadened understanding of scale adds the layer of social construction to its composition and rejects its understanding as an "ontologically given category" (Marston, 2000). Brenner (2001) emphasizes that:

> traditional Euclidian, Cartesian and Westphalian notions of geographic scale as a fixed, bounded, self-enclosed and pregiven container are currently being superseded—at least within the parameter of critical geographical theory and research—by a highly productive emphasis on process, evolution, dynamism and sociopolitical contestation.
>
> (p. 592)

Marston (2000) suggests that scale consists of three, necessarily interrelated components: size, level, and relation. A social construction approach rejects considerations of size (e.g., census tract, zip code, and county) and level (e.g., district, county, and state) as simple categorizations and emphasizes scale as relational within the complexity of space, place, and environment (pp. 220–221). Marsten understands scale in critical analyses as a result of political choices, rooted today within sets of global capitalist relations. Once again we see the recognition that the study of the places we inhabit involves attention to multiple forces at play, interactions within those forces, and the simultaneous blending of the discursive, the affective, and the material.

Neomarxist and cultural studies approaches to spatial analysis developed within critical geography as scholars such as David Harvey, Doreen Massey, and Edward Soja all present global capitalism as a central force within the reconsidered spatial relations. Lefebvre's theorization around the spatial within the post-Fordist global maps an understanding of the ways in which state power connects to the spaces of everyday life. It reminds us too that considering the city as curriculum includes an understanding of the state as its principal author. The spaciocurricular lesson here is in the uneven distribution of varying relationships between citizens and the state.

In Baltimore, we can see a clear example of this process beginning with the redline maps of 1937 (see Map 5). Considerable recent work has traced the racist history of redlining in US urban development (see Rothstein, 2017) and increasingly scholars point to these historical cartographies as the sedimented markers of contemporary inequity. Brenner's (2000) summary of the work of Lefebvre on state power and the construction of scale offers three strategies that can be seen in the case of Baltimore. The redline map clearly shows how regulation, urban planning and policy, and financial investment carve the city into zones either primed for development or cut out of the economic future of the city and is evidence of the states operating "to mobilize space as a productive force." As time goes on and Baltimore readjusts to the decline of Bethlehem Steel, we see the intervention of city planning at the neighborhood scale and in the service of capitalist growth; here the state serves as the "the most crucial *institutional mediator of uneven geographical development*." Finally, we can understand these various types of state intervention in Baltimore as serving to "*hierarchize social relations upon different scales*" and thus creating a spatial logic for the city's policies and practices (emphasis in original, pp. 370–371). Thus, development of a new tourist

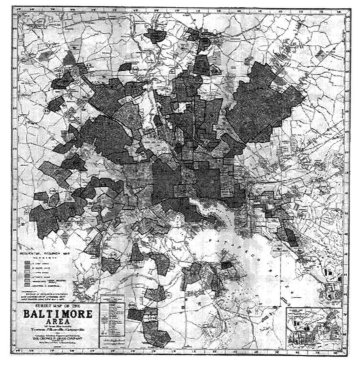

MAP 5   1937 Redline Map: : Residential Security Map of Baltimore, MD (public domain).

destination—the Inner Harbor—for Baltimore and the continued investment in predominately white areas of the city serves to maintain the scalar categories of the redlined city. What Brown (2021) refers to as the "Black butterfly and the White L" represents the spatial legacy of those histories and the ways in which the state (in this case the city) reinforce those borders (see Map 6)

Ansfield (2015) discusses the urban as "the new American frontier, the potentially profitable and undoubtably treacherous landscape whose every street corner gains its meaning from specific modes of racialized thinking derivative of American conquest and subjugation/dismemberment of people of color" (p. 127). Building on the work of Sylvia Wynter, this analysis sees not only economic desires at work in urban planning and policing but historical tropes of purity and habitability coded by racial logic of exclusion. Blackness itself becomes part of the commodification of the new urban core yet it is diffused, limited and "only tolerable when its physical threat is erased, deconcentrated, regulated, and invisibilized" (p. 128). This cartography of humanness marks the spaces and densities allowable as the state remaps the city and, by doing so, creates excluded spaces of possibility for the excess. West Baltimore is one such space and the police killing of Freddie Gray serves as the object lesson of that racist curriculum.

The power structure in Baltimore has designated Sandtown/Winchester as a space of exception—outside of urban renewal, outside of its evolving identity, and outside of its responsibility for social services, education, and due process. The sedimented history of power and politics in Baltimore drew this map and actively reinforced its borders and boundaries. In fact, via Sylvia Wynter (1994), the neighborhood can increasingly be characterized as an NHI space—no

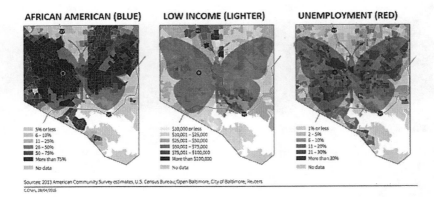

MAP 6 Black Butterfly Maps illustrating Baltimore's socioeconomic differences: (from left to right) the "Black butterfly" and the "White L" (referring to the shapes that the darker and lighter spots on the map create) overlaid by a map of the African-American population, an income map, and an unemployment map. This image was presented by Kristin Baja, Office of Sustainability, City of Baltimore, Maryland in 2018 (NASEM, 2018, p. 78).

humans involved.[2] How else can we make sense of this? For a period of time, I wondered why it was so hard for Democrats or Progressives to say "black lives matter" but I don't anymore; they can't say it because black lives don't matter. They don't matter to so much of the structures acting upon us all. Remember that Freddie Gray ran from the police because he thought they were going to kill him... and they did. So, all of this is to say that we can think of the city as curriculum—it is trying to teach us something—but in this case it is a curriculum of exclusion, of exception, of who matters and who doesn't.

Notes

1 Thanks go to an intentionally anonymous group of authors/activists/advocates for the "Baltimore Black Paper" and these statistics.
2 Sylvia Wynter's powerful reference to the racist procedures of the LAPD after the Rodney King's decision refers to the dehumanization of black people via language, classification, and categorization of people and the state.

7

CONCLUSIONS/CONNECTIONS

The stories presented along the way on this intellectual geography suggest several things about youth and the practice of making place, the spaciocurricular, a scalar approach to social theory, and the process of city shaping. On our first stop, the ways in which the students and staff made place at the William Edenton Learning Lab pointed to the multiplicity and fluidity of spatial intra-actions insisted upon by both critical geographers as well as (I would argue) theorizing with/in the New Materialism. We know that many different stories can be told about places (Harvey, 1996) and the story told here—in this volume—is one influenced in large part by my own position as researcher, former teacher, and constant learner. The spatial analysis presented across these maps begins to think about how students, educators, and communities navigate their own journeys among the forces acting upon them, in the wake of histories laden with meaning, and subsequently making places their own—another step toward a critical geography of education.

Spaces that Silence/Spaces that Speak

Throughout this volume, I have employed the metaphors of mapmaking to point to the analytical emphases enabled by a critical geography. In addition, I point my finger to the lines drawn on the maps of Holden High School, Indianapolis Public Schools, and communities from Macedonia to Baltimore and extend them, pulling them out in a way that places them within sets of relations both historical and global. Maps, like curricula, are exclusionary in nature and this finiteness can certainly be used to silence groups and individuals; they are laden with issues of power, possibility, and material impact. Soja (1989) calls for the increased spatialization of social theory by reminding us that "the organization of space is a social product filled with politics and ideology, contradiction and struggle, comparable to the making of history" (p. 243). In this way, the WELL constitutes only a marginal part of the map (or history) of Holden High School across the street; it also provides a space for those students who attend for the possibility of voice as opposed to silence. The contradiction however lies in how the students—marginalized from the dominant structures of race, class, and geography—took up the WELL and created a place that allows for critique, voice, and even the imagining that something else could be. The resistance to so-called education reform efforts in Indianapolis can be seen as something similar, a contestation over space that, at its core, was fundamentally about whose voices were heard in the re/defining of those educative spaces. The contradiction and struggle of these students and community members—in effect, working to write their own histories—calls for making new maps.

Spaces that Leak

Although the stories across these studies offer up possibilities regarding the rules of class and race for students, educators, and communities, they show how social structures make their way into the places that students themselves largely construct; this is to say that the spaces leak. Schools and other educative spaces are simply not entirely closed or sealed off from these influences. Most prominent in my thoughts regarding the leaky spaces of youth and youth culture is the fact that although I promised myself I would not write a dissertation about Holden High School as I owe the people there much and many friends still teach there, I was unable to approach any story of the WELL without doing so. This in many ways speaks of the particularities of the place of the WELL and my own history and place-making work in coming to know both the WELL and Holden. What we saw was that the context of race and class at Holden leaked into the student's own analysis of the problems at the high school. While another researcher might be able to tell useful stories of the WELL and the students who spend time isolated from the set of relations I call a critical geography, I simply could not.

Spaces of Possibility

Fundamental to this story is the belief, my belief, that there are educative spaces that provide positive things to the students that spend their time there. In early conversations regarding my initial observations of the WELL and the students so actively a part of the vibrant scene, I remember saying that there is "something" there and that it felt profoundly "different" from Holden High School. Related to the aforementioned leaky spaces, the positive effects of spending time at an after-school computer lab—be they feelings of safety, finding of voice, or simply access to a social network—at least have the possibility of leaking back into the spaces of the high school experience. In cities across the United States and across the globe, ideas like equity, democracy, and social justice can also leak into spaces designed specifically to limit those very possibilities. At its heart, the move toward a critical geography is a move toward spatial justice as we recognize that as "the static definitions of the world around us become fluid and where social justice becomes impossible, spaces of possibility emerge" (Huddleston, 2013, p. 114). McKittrick calls for new "more humanly workable geographies" (2006, p. 145) that begin with the dismantling of these oppressive maps and continue with both a recognition of the spatial distribution of alterity, an analysis of how those distribution function and to what end, and a social justice project that takes space seriously. It is in this process of interaction between the places constructed by students, educators, and communities and larger social structures that we can see spaces of possibility. However, we can also see the potential for new, insidious possibilities that marginalize, oppress, and perpetuate inequity and limit access to power.

John Allen argues in *Lost Geographies of Power* that, "reach, proximity and presence are *not* givens; they make a difference to the exercise of power precisely because the many and varied modalities of power are themselves constituted *differently* in space and time" (2003, p. 190). It is in this sense that spaces like the WELL and the education community of Indianapolis are ones of possibility— spaces where students can "get what they need" and organizing and activism can push back on efforts to marginalize and diminish communities of color. The modalities of power and the ways in which they have been constituted in different ways create the conditions for new maps of experience, new conceptions of place. John Allen notes these particularities:

> Through the constant succession of movement and activities, the manner in which they are performed and the style in which they are executed, places take on a life of their own, with certain groups able to superimpose their presence on others. In the entangled nature of people's lives, places, on this account, take their shape through dominant or controlling rhythms that seek to suppress the routine traces of others. Exclusion in this context has less to do with closed doors and high walls, and rather more to do with spaces constructed by dominant groups in their own likeness—through a series of rituals and gestures, moods and attachments, as well as accumulated styles and meanings.
>
> (Allen, 2003, p. 11)

So then, if the *placeness* of schooling establishes social structures that work on the basis of "rituals…gestures, moods, attachments, styles, and meanings" these do not disappear upon crossing the border; they only manifest themselves in a different scale because of changes in reach, proximity, and presence. This again takes us back to the view of the multiplicity of place; places can be present within one another (Massey, 1994, p. 7). I argue that the stories given here are examples of how folk have made place and shaped cities—in multiple ways—that although often in opposition to larger forces at work, still exhibit many of the characteristics evident within the social relations constitutive of particular contexts. Exploring the global city offered much-needed perspective and brought to light significant issues in higher education and the push to internalize the curriculum. But it was Baltimore that provided the reminder of the materiality of exclusion, of how spaces limit possibility, and how the struggle for spatial justice never ends.

Spaces of Resistance/Spaces of Resilience

The argument that students, educators, and communities engage in the processes of making place and shaping cities highlights not only meaning-making but spatial distribution as issues of equity and justice are considered. The mantra that students "get what they need" in these places offers a way to think not only about possibility and hope in educative contexts but also points to the ways in which critical dialogue offers the further possibility for spaces of resistance. Opening up spaces for youth to define the parameters of their interactions for themselves and to analyze the strictures acting upon them becomes the political project. Globally, we see how those pushed to the political and economic margins will find and/or create these spaces as well, be they soccer pitches or public radio. The question however becomes, is this indeed resistance with possibility or, rather merely another form of social reproduction? To decide, some clarification is in order.

Social Reproduction

The process of social reproduction holds the prominent position in the work of critical theorists who emphasize schools and educative environments. In particular, these theorists struggle to understand how issues of social class transfer over generational lines within the structures of schools and curriculum. McLaren (1994) offers that the work of critical theory in education resides in the "explor[ing of] how schools perpetuate or reproduce the social relationships and attitudes needed to sustain existing dominant economic and class relations of the larger society" (p. 194). Willis (1977) contributed greatly to this project in the germinal *Learning to Labor*. In his study, the "lads" employed normative notions of masculinity to justify their rejection of behaviors that would lead to academic success. Reacting to the class bias in their social context, their efforts at resistance only reinforced the processes of social reproduction. In other words, taking the lead from Paul Willis, how working-class kids become working-class adults despite their rejection of dominant ideology and efforts to resist.

Bowles and Gintis (1976, 2001) argue that class position in American society directly determines achievement and responsiveness to schooling experiences. In essence they argue that schooling itself exists to place people within their appropriate role in a capitalist society. What they deem the "Correspondence Principle" states that the combination of a subservient workforce constructed through the rewarded behaviors of docility and compliance, an unquestioning acceptance of hierarchical structures, and the reinforcing culture of external rewards—grades, diplomas, wages, promotions—produce school subjects that have been prepared for the world of work. While telling in its analysis of a factor in social reproduction, correspondence theory fails to take into account both resistance and resilience in student behaviors. Giroux (1983a, 1983b) strives to use an emphasis on the operations of culture to better understand how students come in conflict with and resist the dominant forces at work in schools. Defining a Resistance Theory as "represent[ing] an important terrain in the ideological battle for the appropriation of meaning and experience...it provides educators with an opportunity to link the political with the personal in order to understand how power is mediated, resisted, and reproduced in daily life" (1983b, p. 293).

At the WELL, Emily resists the status markers of fashion and class by openly flaunting her transgression and also by claiming the place of the WELL as one in which those markers that serve to establish dominance at the high school actually mark exclusion. Further, her distaste for the racial politics of the hallways of Holden and their inappropriateness at the WELL sets up a different standard for how race is performed in those extended borders. For Mathew and Todd—two white students who skirt the borders of inclusion at Holden—the resistance offered at the WELL lies in their ability to still attain the social capital of extracurricular activities for college applications without having to struggle through the rigid hierarchy of the high school's clubs and activities. As the WELL enables a shifting in and out of its parameters, the young men are also able to engage in the other activities offered to the "WELL family" without having to justify their participation to their peers. They are allowed to take up the WELL when they so desire and leave it behind, even eliminate it from their social self when those students outside the borders might not understand the WELL's utility, meaning, or even character. In fact, the two white boys are enabled to participate in the activities of spaces defined as "black" by the dominant culture of the high school.

Lily and Amy both identify their ability to help other students with technological aspects of the lab as their reasons for staying at the WELL. Amy, in moralistic overture, suggests that students with fewer advantages than her need the services and skill development offered at the WELL. She states that she "wants to impact people" and touts a color-blind approach that holds much more compassion and respect for the patrons than the male staffers. She seems to revel in this position of difference, going so far as to almost identify herself with the phrase, "this is where I differ." Lily, speaking explicitly of the technology facilities of the WELL, betrays an interest in the male staffers that share her aesthetic and taste in music. She researches the life of Kurt Cobain and flirts with the boy prone to Clash t-shirts. As Todd described the WELL as an "outsiders kind of thing...they invite the different," Lily seems to be coming to the lab to find the "different" that she can identify with. Lily interestingly stops short of taking up the WELL as an identity—as only the staffers partly do—by noting that playing volleyball prevents her from year-round attendance. She takes up the WELL when she needs it.

Sharia and Ward resist much of the constraints of Holden High School and seem to approach the WELL as the place to vent on the absurdities of the school day. So much so do they guard the place they have worked to construct that when time came for my formal interview they shut down, fearing that to speak with the microphone on would reveal their secret and jeopardize the character of the WELL. Outside of that refusal, they participate importantly in the YMCA meeting critiquing both race relations at Holden and what they see as feeble attempts by that group to address them.

These stories do indeed link the political aspects of students navigating social groups, race relations, college admissions, and even well-intentioned liberals with the very personal aspects of their lives such as safety, mobility, and belonging. It is the place of the WELL, and more importantly the ability of students to collectively construct that place that enables this resistance to the exclusionary structures of school for these kids.

Economies of Identity

As this volume begins with the question of what is "different" about the place of the WELL, it becomes necessary to highlight what students do *not* do at the lab in relation to other studies of students and place. Eckert (1989) notes how students in American high schools territorialize their school spaces based on social groupings. A series of normative behaviors (style, clothing, language) serve to mark these territories as belonging to one of the two dominant youth groups—in her terms, "jocks and burnouts." Nespor (1997) maps how students divide elementary classroom space in terms of normative gender and broader social roles, pointing to how children use place to engage in gender and racial boundary work. The transgression of those boundaries by students, teachers, and he as researcher—introducing another aspect of power in the relations—enter into the children's continual construction of those boundaries and add to the mix of how they make meaning out of them. Reminiscent of the geographer John Allen's depiction of the development of place through dominant codes and behaviors, Eckert and Nespor describe the reflexive nature of place and identity as access to certain school spaces serves to mark student identities within school cultures. This type of analysis has been furthered by scholars investigating queer spaces, indigenous places, black aesthetics of place, and other critical approaches to taking space seriously. In other words, presence in certain places often comes to symbolize a person's position within the social structure and ultimately provides social networks (good or bad) that extend beyond schooling into the larger society.

Students at the WELL specifically do *not* use the WELL for identity purposes across the street at Holden High School but community activists in Indianapolis claim spaces as their own and refuse to see a complicated history erased. The students cross the border and return to the complex of social structures at work at their high school; they leave the identity forms used at the WELL behind and in effect, create an economy of identities. Activists too claim identities rooted in notions of place and actively embark on city shaping, in formal and informal ways. As highlighted throughout this volume, people embark in efforts to get "what they need" but not necessarily to claim identity forms that translate into the social hierarchy across the metaphorical or literal street. In these cases—and when it's possible—actors take up place-based identities to get what they need but just as easily leave those same forms by the wayside.

The way students used the WELL differs notably from the divisions marked by Eckert and Nespor when the scale of analysis expands to include both school and WELL. Instead of working on spaces to define them and conversely allowing their own identity forms to be marked by their presence in those places, the students who participated at the WELL entered the place already in opposition to the norms of Holden and use it to get what they need—specifically to help them navigate the structures at work at the school. To narrow the focus to only the borders of the lab, only the elite are excluded and it seems largely by their own sense of the altered rules of race, class, and difference. These practices served as strategies that help students negotiate their lives in relation to the forces that are at work upon them. The WELL offers these students a way to work around reproduction and not only come to resistance, but resilience. In similar ways, we can see how folk in Baltimore and Indianapolis use spaces and their entanglement with them as part of their own strategies of resistance and resilience but, in turning our eye to the spatial we can uncover the ways in spaces are employed in attempts to limit that very work.

The mapmakers working today that I am most excited about are black and indigenous women. The works of Katharine McKittrick (2006) and Tiffany Lethobo King (2019) both pull back the layers of racialized space and layer on top of new geographies of black bodies and the ways in which they experience the world. McKittrick points to the processes of spatial production and the influence of race and racism, but as she focuses on the lives of women of color, she highlights place making from the margins and the cracks in the structure. Only because such spatial practices are ignored, obscured, or marginalized by society writ large is it that we don't see the value of these spaces and what they represent. Indeed, as McKittrick and scholars like her point out, these spaces hold critical importance in the lives of people of color and encourage us to imagine spaces differently. This work points to a spatial production that is inherently about a broader social justice project. King (2019) expands on exactly these ideas and further connects to the work of Sylvia Wynter. She notes how the category of the human has been historically denied to both black and indigenous peoples and how that is evidenced in a spatially represented world. Critiques of coloniality and future desire for the celebration of black embodiment mark a new cartography that interrupts the legacies of the colonial project and white supremacy. These projects not only help in the thinking through the spaciocurricular but also, most certainly, point to new spaces of possibility.

In a remarkable chapter in a book on the displacement and gentrification efforts in Washington, D.C., Summer (2019) suggests that "the Corner" is a useful way to think about the intersection of race, space, and the urban. Her analysis of a particular corner (Eight and H streets in D.C.) also points to a framing that can be seen in Raleigh, Indianapolis, and Baltimore. She notes the ways that blackness is spatialized, "imagining the role of geography in the production of blackness and the concurrent structuring of space through the aesthetic emplacement of blackness" (pp. 144–145). Seeing the Corner as not just a space waiting for gentrification, Summer suggests that the racialized meaning of the place holds much more nuanced components such as issues of transit and employment, surveillance and visibility, and an aesthetic that only tentatively allows for a public blackness. As narratives of inclusion and diversity permeate efforts at urban development, "blackness—as a representation of difference—should be explicitly visible. The containment of Black presence at the Corner makes blackness less intimidating, since the representation of blackness is intimately reduced to the body" (p. 147). Here we see the complex and contradictory nature of race and place in contemporary contexts but, we can also note these operations as following Lefebvre's understanding of the state and spatial production. Where black presence in white spaces was openly contested in Indianapolis, West Baltimore's exclusion from urban development allowed other sectors of the city to be remapped. In different ways and not unlike the lesson of the Corner, both are examples of spatial, racial containment.

Insisting upon close attention to the *materiality* of education policy—the lived experience of schools or what can be referred to as sociomaterial—and approaching the work through a radical contextuality that seeks to place ideological and cultural forces in context, this cultural studies/critical geography approach to education takes up both the political project of imagining new possibilities as well as understanding school and schooling as much more than simple, bounded systems. The future/present of curriculum theory and cultural studies of education should be precisely to continue the conversation that takes seriously the cultural production of meaning around issues of education, the ethical commitments of academic analysis, the ways in which the remapped urban space is written on people and communities, as well as continuing within the hope for new, undiscovered possibilities. As this intellectual geography was an attempt to move toward a critical geography of education framework, further inquiry could certainly be done to try and understand the multiple trajectories of power working on kids, schools, and communities. As mentioned in defining critical geography, issues of changing economic structures, globalization, and ideological conflict all affect those spending time in spaces. To fully realize a critical geography, one would need to expand the analysis to include all of those complexities and theorize on how they impact place and place-making. The work here represents the opening steps of that journey and attempts to show a corner of the map of an intellectual geography. What spaces try to teach us, or as I've called it here, the spaciocurricular, offers another angle of vision, another thread to pull in the untangling of the knot that is making sense of the world. I have found it helpful to remember—and perhaps you will too, the words of de Certeau (1984, p.129), that "what the map cuts up, the story cuts across". Thanks for coming along.

8

NOTES ON METHOD

Inquiry into how people create and negotiate space, place, power, and identity necessarily calls forth a qualitative approach. How space and place are constructed within domains of discursive, affective, material, and power-laded forces fits within a broader conception of education as fluid, dynamic interaction between students, educators, communities, and world. A way to describe this interaction necessarily includes the perceptions of the people involved as well as those of the researcher looking in. This is not to say that other research methods are without value, but rather to stress that particular methods serve particular purposes. Quantitative methods can often provide new insights into the effectiveness of programs, descriptive understandings of educational efforts, and potentially suggest areas in need of improvement. However, schools are not factories and students are not products. The complexities of human interaction require a complex way of coming to know and telling the tale.

Postcritical Ethnography

The empirical work included in this volume and the studies that influenced the theoretical trajectories here come from a methodological commitment rooted in contemporary ethnography. Like postmodernism and poststructuralism, postcritical ethnography is not the antithesis of critical ethnography but, rather requires the tools of critique be applied to ethnographic inquiry itself (see Noblit, Flores, & Murillo, 2004). Quantz (1992) suggests several definitions of critical ethnography that all basically refuse to dichotomize theory and method. Specifically, "critical ethnography's contribution to this dialogue lies principally in its ability to make concrete the particular manifestations of marginalized cultures located in a broader sociopolitical framework" (p. 462). Arguing that critical ethnography in education comes out of dissatisfaction with trends in sociology of education that served to apologize for the status quo (p. 451), or to romanticize the deviant serving only to see victimization (p. 453), Quantz suggests that critical ethnography in education begins with Paul Willis' groundbreaking study *Learning to Labor* (1977, p. 455). Carspecken (1996), in the effort toward a clearer definition, suggests that critical ethnography consists of researchers with both a particular orientation of values and a critical epistemology. The values espoused by such researchers include a critique of the social and the cultural, opposition to inequality, the project of revealing structures of oppression in all of its forms, and the equalization of power relations (pp. 6–7). Furthermore, the critical epistemology of the work demands an explicit recounting of the ways in which the presentation of findings, claims of validity, and representation of reality are all embedded within relations of power (Madison, 2012). Understanding how the construction of knowledge itself is an act of power puts the researchers in the bind of both speaking to inequity in power relations while bringing to light their own privilege in that construction (Noblit, Flores, & Murillo, 2004, p. 185). Postcritical ethnography then is an explicit attempt to rearticulate such dual moves.

In the attempt to get at the question of "did we get it right?" (Erickson, 1993; Stake, 1995) many researchers have embraced the notion of including the participants themselves in the analysis of the qualitative data collected. In essence, studies include a component that asks those in the study to reflect on the study itself and participate in the construction of knowledge. Using what Gitlin and Russell (1994) call Educative Research, this project seeks to include the participants in a dialogical process that "negotiate[s] meaning" at all levels of the inquiry. In this way the voices of the students and staff involved in the study were brought to the fore which, in turn, served to change the trajectories of the inquiry and shaped the stories told in particular ways. This necessary move however does not inoculate the researcher from the dangers or misrepresentation, the ethical challenges to working with vulnerable populations, or the "failure coming to know" in every project (Childers, 2011, p. 353).

From this changing relationship between researcher and participants also comes the call for educational research as agent for social change. Erickson (1993) makes a call for a reciprocal circuit of knowledge, in effect working both ways. In this way "teacher research is a form of social change wherein individuals and groups labor to understand and alter classrooms, schools, and school communities" and "makes visible the ways teachers and students co-construct knowledge and curriculum" (Erickson, 1993). Some in qualitative research see the inclusion of multiple voices, changing power relations, and a critical approach to schools and society, as the possibility for a democratic politics inherent in the work. O'Brian (2000) sees the new paradigm of qualitative research as challenging educators at multiple levels to "understand the moral and ethical dimensions of educational practice" (O'Brian, 2000). Therefore, not only does the inquiry acknowledge the subjectivity of both facilitator and participant, it explicitly tried to use that subjectivity for social change.

The aim of the study of the WELL (Chapters 2 and 3, this volume) was to explore the perceptions of students who attend the WELL regarding their reasons for participation, goals, and intentions for their time spent there, and their relationship to the technology opportunities offered. Thus, the qualitative research methodology included individual interviews (Kvale, 1996), classroom and participant observation (Denzin & Lincoln, 2000) and participant research models (Price, 2001; Rogers, Noblit, & Ferrel 1999). Member checking through the levels of the analysis followed the intent of an action research model, resulting (to a certain degree) in a collaborative effort between researcher and participant. Central to the methodology of this work was the explicit intention to minimize power and status differentials between facilitator and participant (Madison, 2019; see also Cannella & Lincoln, 2012). As much as possible the project itself was seen as a co-inquiry with the questions and interests of the students placed in a position of privilege. Although early in the methodological journey of this researcher, the intent was a beginning step toward "more complex and rich pictures of the contexts we study—a movement that includes retaining a firm regard for the personal, individual, and other complex contexts that inform our work—[and] adds to depth and richness of questions asked, the findings co-authors present, as well as the processes of data collection and analysis utilized to arrive at such findings" (Gershon, 2009, p. xviii).

Privileging student voice and allowing the students to "check" my analysis at various points during the research necessarily changed the trajectory of the study. This is to say that this study moved, both in variation from the original aims and in the recognition that there is not one story of the WELL but a polyphony. It is important to note that what followed was an emergent qualitative design—the questions going in to this study were not the same as the ones at the end of the inquiry. Recognizing that preconceived notions of the researcher can influence the outcome, operationalize the procedure, and distort the findings (Carspecken (1996), p. 25), guiding questions were used in this study as more of a point of departure, leaving the door open to the directions in which student responses would take the study. Therefore, while relevant to the project as a whole, pieces of this method reflected the broadly painted intentions of the project, conceived 2 years ago in isolation, while others reflected the new and emergent trajectories garnered from interactions with the months with the students themselves.

In light of those preliminary interviews and interactions, the primary goal of this study was to explore the ways in which the students who attend the after-school programs of the William Edenton Learning Lab have created an alternative sense of community in response to the normative social structures of the adjacent high school and their urban home communities. It was proposed that the spatial relationships of home/school, school/not-school, and WELL—as liminal space between home and communities students themselves construct—formed a way in which to understand how students create identity forms in complex and fluid ways. Therefore, a theoretical framework based in critical geography served as an analytic tool in coming to understand the interviews and observations of the researcher.

Realizing another connection between the fields of education and cultural studies, postcritical ethnography offers an alternative methodology to scholars of color who refuse the ways in which critical ethnography continue to "recreate both the center and border as it wishes to speak for people of color" (Noblit, 1999, p. 5). Noblit et al. (2004) compare these trajectories in education with the "new ethnography" in cultural studies (see Grossberg, Nelson, & Treichler, 1992), described as the means for scholars exploring issues of social and cultural reproduction. Postcritical research areas that embrace the study of postcolonialism, feminisms, and the critical study of race and ethnicity all seek to expose the researchers own positionality and whatever forms of privilege that might arise from those subject positions. Connections with participants are highlighted rather than obscured in a postcritical ethnography and in such a work there is a recognition that in studying the "other" we, in effect, learn about "us" (Noblit, 1999; see also Nieto, 1999). However, the question remains as to the role of the spatial in both these interactions and their subsequent analysis.

Also, it is hoped, that my own voice as author and researcher in this text is both "muted and clear" (Fine & Weis, 1998, p. 14). I come to this study as a former teacher at the attendant high school—the "cool one" as I am described by the students of the WELL who knew me, a participant in the activities of the WELL, and as person from the university. All of the aforementioned put me in particular relations with the students with which I interacted. This study tried to center the voices of those students in the hopes of bringing their particularities to the conversation revolving around schools, schooling, and the ways in which young people negotiated those structures. However, my own voice as researcher was clear in that my allegiances lie with these kids that find themselves in "the divide"—outside the norms of social hierarchy, academic success, and even home community. Thus I, like these students, straddled and navigated, and ultimately crossed, a number of borders when at the WELL.

This then leads to the method for this study and the work that followed. Critical ethnography often leaves out more complex questions of relations and interactions both within the negotiations of the participants and between the researcher and the object studied. So then, while embracing the overtly political project of critical ethnography, my empirical work has sought out to add the "post," the "yes, but..." to the method. Postcritical ethnography seeks to address questions of positionality, objectivity, reflexivity, and representation (Noblit 2004). The discourses of postmodernism, postcolonialism, affect and critical race theory all serve to challenge traditional notions of both ethnographic work and ethnographers themselves. A researcher's position and identity matter within the confines of the study itself. To assume that one could objectively observe and write the "true story" of any particular set of relations no longer holds.

Thus, a critical geography framework in qualitative research provides an opportunity to interrogate both the spatial construction of educative spaces and the place-making practices of the students, educators, and community members, who cross the street—the border—to spend time there. Within this theoretical frame, the stories they tell reflect both their sense of place, the spatial forces at work on them, the divides they cross, negotiate, reinscribe, and the politics of social formations both within and without institutionalized spaces. Those stories also point us to the material aspects of the spatial and uncover the ways in which they act upon people and the process of meaning-making. The negotiation of those spaces and the processes of mapping placed onto those terrains serve as the focus of a critical geography project. In so doing, further untangling the web of practices of educative spaces helps us see these interactions from a different vantage point and enables us to remap our conceptions of education itself.

REFERENCES

Agamben, G. (2005). *State of Exception*. Chicago: University of Chicago Press.

Aitken, S. (2001). *Geographies of young people: The morally contested spaces of identity*. New York: Routledge.

Alexander, K., Entwistle, D., & Olson, L. (2014). *The long shadow: Family background, disadvantaged urban youth, and the transition to adulthood*. New York: Russel Sage Foundation.

Allen, J. (2003). *Lost geographies of power*. Malden, MA: Blackwell Publishing.

Ansfield, B. (2015). Still submerged: The uninhabitability of urban redevelopment. In K. McKittrick (Ed.) *Sylvia Wynter: On being human as praxis*. Durham: Duke University Press.

Anzaldua, G. (1987). *Borderlands/La Frontera: The new mestiza*. San Francisco: Spinsters/Aunt Lute.

Ayscue, J. B., Flaxman, G., Kuscera, J., & Siegal-Hawley, G. (2013). "Settle for Segregation or Strive for Diversity? A Defining Moment for Maryland's Public Schools." *Civil Rights Project/Proyecto Derechos Civiles*. Retrieved from https://www.civilrightsproject.ucla.edu/research/k-12-education/integration-and-diversity/settle-for-segregation-or-strive-for-diversity-a-defining-moment-for-maryland2019s-public-schools.

Barad, K. (2007). *Meeting the universe halfway: Quantum physics and the entanglement of matter and meaning*. Durham, NC: Duke University Press.

Battimer, A. (1993). *Geography and the human spirit*. Baltimore, MD: John Hopkins University Press.

Bayor, R.H. (1996). *Race and the shaping of twentieth-century Atlanta*. Chapel Hill, NC: University of North Carolina Press.

Bhabha, H. (1994). *Location of Culture*. New York: Routledge.

Blockett, R. (2017). 'I think it's very much placed on us': Black queer men laboring to forge community at a predominately White and (hetero)cisnormative research institution. *International Journal of Qualitative Studies in Education* 30(8), 800–816.

Bowles, S. & Gintis, H. (1976). *Schooling in capitalist America*. New York: Basic Books.

Bowles, S. & Gintis, H. (2001). *Schooling in capitalist America revisited*. Retrieved June 14, 2004, from http://www.umass.edu/preferen/gintis/soced.pdf.

Breitbart, M. M. (1998). 'Dana's Mystical Tunnel': Young people's designs for survival and change in the city. In T. Skelton & G. Valentine (Eds.), *Cool places: Geographies of youth cultures*. New York: Routledge.

Brenner, N. (1997). Global, fragmented, hierarchical: Henri Lefebvre's geographies of globalization. *Public Culture* 10(1), pp. 135–167.

Brenner, N. (2000). The urban question as a scale question: Reflections on Henri Lefebvre, urban Theory and the politics of scale. *International Journal of Urban and Regional Research* 24(2), 361–378.

Brenner, N. (2001). The limits to scale? Methodological reflections on scalar structuration. *Progress in Human Geography* 25(4), 591–614.

Brenner, N. & Elden, S. (Eds.) (2009). *State, space, world: Selected essays by Henri Lefebvre*. Minneapolis, MN: University of Minneapolis Press.

Brown, L. T. (2015). Down to the Wire: Displacement and Disinvestment in Baltimore City. In T. Rone (Ed.) *The 2015 State of Black Baltimore*. Baltimore: The Greater Baltimore Urban League.

Brown, L.T. (2021). *The black butterfly: The harmful politics of race and space in America*. Baltimore, MD: Johns Hopkins University Press.

Buendía, E. (2010). Reconsidering the urban in Urban Education: Interdisciplinary conversations. *Urban Review*, 43(1), 1–21.

Buendía, E. & Ares, N. (2006). *Geographies of difference: The social production of the east side, west side, and central city school*. New York: Peter Lang.

Buendía, E., Ares, N., Juarez, B. G., & Peercy, M. (2004, March 8). The geographies of difference: The production of the East Side, West Side, and Central City School. *American Educational Research Journal*, 41(4), 833–863.

Cannella, G.S. & Lincoln, Y.S. (2012). Deploying qualitative methods for critical social purposes. In Steinberg, S.R. & Cannella, G.S. (Eds.) *Critical qualitative research reader*. New York: Peter Lang, 104–115.

Carspecken, P. F. (1996) *Critical Ethnography in Educational Research; A Theoretical and Practical Guide*. New York and London: Routledge.

Charteris, J., Smardon, D., Foulkes, R., & Bewley, S. (2016). Heterarchical coaching for continuing teacher professional learning and development: a transversal analysis of agency. *International Journal of Qualitative Studies in Education* 30(6): 546–559. 10.1080/09518398.2016.1265688

Charteris, J., Smardon, D., Foulkes, R. & Bewley, S. (2017) Heterarchical coaching for continuing teacher professional learning and development: A transversal analysis of agency. *International Journal of Qualitative Studies in Education*, 30(6), 546–559, doi: 10.1080/09518398.2016.1265688

Childers, S. M. (2011). Getting in trouble: Feminist postcritical policy ethnography in an urban school. *Qualitative Inquiry*, 17(4) 345–354.

Childress, L. K. (2010). *The Twenty-first century university: Developing faculty engagement in internationalization*. New York: Peter Lang.

Cobb, C. D. (2020). Geospatial analysis: A new window into educational equity, access, and opportunity. *Review of Research in Education*, 44(1), 97–129.

Crenson, M.A. (2017). *Baltimore: A political history*. Baltimore, MD: Johns Hopkins University Press.

Davies, W. & Gilmartin, M. (2002). Geography as a cultural field. In Gerber, R. and Williams, M. (Eds.) *Geography, culture and education*, (13–30). Boston, MA: Kluwer Academic.

De Certeau, M. (1984). *The practice of everyday life*. Berkeley, University of California Press.

De Certeau, M., Mayol, P., & Tomasik, T. (1998). In L. Giard, (Ed.) *Practice of everyday life: Volume 2: Living and cooking*. Minneapolis, MN: University of Minnesota Press.

Delanty, G. (2003). *Community*. New York: Routledge.

Denzin, N.K. & Lincoln, Y.S., (Eds.) (2000). *Handbook of qualitative research*, 2nd edition. Thousand Oaks: Sage Publications.

Dimitriadis, G. & Carlson, D. (Eds.). (2003). *Promises to keep: Cultural studies, democratic education, and public life*. New York: Routledge Falmer.

Eckert, P. (1989). *Jocks & burnouts: Social categories and identity in the high school*. New York: Teachers College Press.

Edwards, G. (2001). A very British subject: Questions of identity. In D. Lambert & P. Machon (Eds.), *Citizenship through secondary geography* (pp. 109–121). London and New York: Routledge.

Ellis, J. (2004). The significance of place in the curriculum of children's everyday lives. *Taboo: The Journal of Culture and Education*, 8(1), 23–42.

Erickson, F. (1993). Foreward. In M. Cochran-Smith & S. Lytle (Eds.) *Inside/Outside: Teacher research and knowledge*. New York: Teachers College Press.

Fataar, A. (2013). Students' bodily carvings in school spaces of the post-apartheid city. *Taboo: The Journal of Culture and Education*, 13(1), 11–20.

Fataar, A. (2019). Turning space into place: The place-making practices of school girls their informal spaces of their high school. *Research in Education* 104(1), 24–42.

Fine, M. & Weis, L. (1998). *The unknown city: The lives of poor and working-class young adults*. Boston: Beacon Press.

Foucault, M. (1980), Questions on Geography. In C. Gordon, (Ed.), *Power/Knowledge: Selected Interviews and Other Writings 1972–1977*, (pp. 63–77). New York: Pantheon Books.

Foucault, M. (1994a). Governmentality. In J. Faubion, (Ed.) *Power* (pp. 201–223). New York: The New Press.

Foucault, M. (1994b). Interview with Michel Foucault. In J. Faubion (Ed.) *Power* (pp. 239–297). New York: The New Press.

Foucault, M., & Miskowiec, J. (1986). Of Other Spaces. *Diacritics*, 16(1), 22–27. doi:10.2307/464648

Francis, L., & Munson, M.M. (2016). We help each other up: Indigenous scholarship, survivance, tribalography, and sovereign activism. *International Journal of Qualitative Studies in Education*, 30(1), 48–57. 10.1080/09518398.2016.1242807

Friedel, T. (2014). Outdoor education as a site of epistemological persistence: Unsettling an understanding of urban indigenous youth resistance. In Tuck, E. & Yang, K.W. (Eds.). *Youth resistance research and theories of change*. New York, Routledge, 195–208.

Friedman, T. (1999). *The Lexus and the olive tree: Understanding globalization*. New York: Farrar, Straus and Giroux.

Friere, P. (1970). *Pedagogy of the oppressed*. New York: Continuum.

Geertz, C. (1973). *The interpretation of cultures*. New York, Harper Collins.

Gerber, R. & Lidstone, J. (1996). *Developments and directions in geographical education*. Clevedon: ChannelView Publications.

Gershon, W. S. (2009). Introduction: Working together in qualitative research—the many faces of collaboration. In W. Gershon (Ed.). *The collaborative turn: Working together in qualitative research*. Boston, MA: Sense Publishers.

Gershon, W. S. (2017). Sonic cartography: Mapping space, place, race and identity in an urban middle school. *Taboo: The Journal of Culture and Education*, 13(1), 21–45. Retrieved from http://freireproject.org/wpcontent/journals/taboo/vol13_files/07gershon.pdf

Gershon, W. S. (2018). *Sound curriculum: Sonic studies in educational theory, method, and practice.* New York: Routledge.

Gibson-Graham, J. K. (2003). An ethics of the local. *Rethinking Marxism*, 15(1), 49–74.

Gieryn, T. (2000). A space for place in sociology. *Annual Review of Sociology, 26*, 463–496. Retrieved February 26, 2021, from http://www.jstor.org/stable/223453

Giroux, H. (1983a). *Theory and resistance: A pedagogy for the opposition.* South Hadley, MA: Bergin and Garvey Publishers.

Giroux, H. (1983b). Theories of reproduction and resistance in the New Sociology of Education: A critical analysis. *Harvard Educational Review* 53(3), pp. 257–293.

Giroux, H. A. (2000). *Impure acts: The practical politics of cultural studies.* New York: Routledge.

Gitlin, A. and Russell, R. (1994). Alternative methodologies and the research context. In *Power and method: Political activism and educational research. A. Gitlin.* New York: Routledge, 181–202.

Gough, N. (2004). Editorial: A vision for transnational curriculum inquiry. *Transnational Curriculum Inquiry* 1(1), 1–11.

Graham, J.K.G. and Roelvink, G. (2010), An economic ethics for the anthropocene. *Antipode*, 41: 320–346. doi:10.1111/j.1467-8330.2009.00728.x

Grande, S. & McCarty, T.L. (2018). Indigenous elsewheres: Refusal and re-membering in education research, policy, and praxis. *International Journal of Qualitative Studies in Education*, 31(3), 165–167. doi:10.1080/09518398.2017.1401144

Gregory, D. (1978). *Ideology, science and human geography.* London: Hutchinson.

Gregory, D. (1994) *Geographical Imaginations.* Oxford: Blackwell.

Grossberg, L. (2005). *Caught in the crossfire: Kids, politics, and America's future.* Boulder, Colorado: Paradigm Publishers

Grossberg, L., Nelson, C. & Treichler, P. (1992). *Cultural studies.* New York: Routledge.

Gruenewald, D. (2003). The best of both worlds: A critical pedagogy of place. *Educational Researcher*, 32(4), 3–12.

Gulson, K.N. & Symes, C. (2007) Knowing one's place: Space, theory, education, *Critical Studies in Education*, 48(1), 97–110. doi:10.1080/17508480601123750

Gupta, A. & Ferguson, J. (1992). Beyond 'culture': Space, identity and the politics of difference. *Cultural Anthropology*, **7**(1), 6–23.

Hardt, M. & Negri, A (2000) *Empire.* Cambridge, MA: Harvard University Press.

Hardt, M. & Negri, A (2004) *Multitude: War and democracy in the age of empire.* London: Penguin.

Harvey, D. (1973). *Social justice and the city.* Baltimore: Johns Hopkins University Press.

Harvey, D. (1989). *The condition of postmodernity: An enquiry into the origins of cultural change.* Cambridge, MA: Basil Blackwell.

Harvey, D. (1996). *Justice, nature and the geography of difference.* Cambridge, MA: Blackwell.

Harvey, D. (2001). *Spaces of capital: Towards a critical geography.* New York: Routledge.

Harvey, D. (2005). *Spaces of neoliberalization: Towards a theory of uneven geographical development.* Munchen, Germany: Franz Steiner Verlag.

Helfenbein, R. (2005). *The urbanization of everything: Thoughts on Globalization and Education.* Unpublished paper presented at the *1st Annual Conference on Globalization, Diversity, and Education Conference*, Pullman, WA, March 3–5, 2005.

Helfenbein, R. (2006a). Economies of identity: Cultural studies and a curriculum of making place. *Journal of Curriculum Theorizing* 22(2), 87–100.

Helfenbein, R. (2006b). A critical geography of youth culture. In Steinberg, S.R., P. Parmar, & B. Richard (Eds.). *Contemporary youth culture: An international encyclopedia* (pp.21–24).Westport, CT: Greenwood Press.

Helfenbein, R. J. (2011a). Thinking through scale: Critical geography and curriculum spaces. In E. Malewski (Ed.), *Curriculum studies handbook:The next moment* (pp. 304–317). New York: Routledge.

Helfenbein, R. (2011b). The urbanization of everything: Thoughts on globalization and education. In S.Tozer, B. Gallegos & A. Henry (Eds.). *Handbook of research in social foundations of education.* New York: Routledge, 319–326.

Helfenbein, R. (2012). New meridians: Social education and citizenship in a critical geography. In T. Kenreich (Ed.) *Geography and social justice in the classroom.* New York: Routledge, 150–160.

Helfenbein, R. (2015). Geographical milieu. M. F. He, B. Schultz & W. Schubert (Eds.) *The SAGE guide to curriculum in education.* Los Angeles, CA: SAGE.

Helfenbein, R. & Buendia, E. (2017). Critical Geographies of education:Theoretical framework. In Ares, N., Buendia, E., Helfenbein, R. (Eds.). *Deterritorializing/Reterritorializing: Critical geography of educational reform.* Sense Publishers, pp. 27–39.

Helfenbein, R. & Clauser, K. (2008).What maps try to teach us. [Review of the book Digital Geography: Geospatial Technologies in the Social Studies Classroom]. *Theory and Research in Social Education* 36(4), 447–452.

Helfenbein, R. & Gonzalez-Velez,Y. (2005). Urban middle school faculty and perceptions of place. In J.A.Anderson, M.J. Dare & K.M. Powell (Eds.), *The urban education inquiry project.* Indianapolis, IN: Center for Urban and Multicultural Education.

Helfenbein, R., & Taylor, L. H. (2009). Critical geographies in/of education: Introduction. *Educational Studies*, 45(3), 236–239.

Hubbard, P., Kitchin, R., & Valentine, G. (Eds.) (2004). *Key thinkers on space and place.* Thousand Oaks, CA: Sage Publications.

Huddleston, G. (2013). Thinking spatially and moving towards the material: a essay on seeking spatial justice by Edward Soja. *Taboo: The Journal of Culture and Education*, 13 (1). doi:10.31390/taboo.13.1.09.

Hultin, L. (2019). On becoming a sociomaterial researcher: Exploring epistemological practices grounded in relational, performative ontology. *Information and Organization* 29(1), 91–104.

Hutchison, D. (2004). *A natural history of place in education.* New York: Teachers College Press.

Hytten, K. (1999).The promise of cultural studies in education. *Educational Theory*, 49(4). 527–543.

IFF (2013).The shared challenge of quality schools:A place-based analysis of school performance in Indianapolis. Retreived September 20, 2013 from http://www.iff.org/ research

Johnson, N. B. (1982). School spaces and architecture:The social and cultural landscape of educational environments. *Journal of American Culture* 5(4). 79–88.

Kern, L. (2020). *Feminist city: Claiming space in a man-made world.* Brooklyn, NY:Verso.

Kincheloe, J. (2001). *Getting beyond the facts:Teaching social studies/social sciences in the twenty-first century.* New York: Peter Lang.

Kincheloe, J. & Pinar, W. (Eds.) *Curriculum as social psychoanalysis: The significance of place.* Alabany, NY: State University of New York Press.

King,T. L. (2019). *The Black shoals: Offshore formations of Black and Native Studies.* Durham, NC: Duke University Press.

Kitchens, J. & Helfenbein, R. (2005). *Curriculum as critical geography: Space, place, and education*. Unpublished paper presented at the *Annual Meeting of the American Association for the Advancement of Curriculum Studies*, Montreal, Canada.

Kliebard, H. (2004). *The struggle for the American curriculum, 1893–1958*. New York, NY: Routledge Falmer.

Kvale, S. (1996). *InterViews*. Thousand Oaks, CA: Sage Publications.

Lambert, D. & Machon, P. (eds) (2001) *Citizenship through secondary geography*. London: Routledge Falmer

Lefebvre, H. (1991). *The production of space*. Oxford: Basil Blackwell.

Lefebvre, H. (2003/1970). *The urban revolution*. Minneapolis, MN: University of Minnesota Press.

Levine, M. (1987), Downtown redevelopment as an urban growth strategy: A critical appraisal of the Baltimore renaissance. *Journal of Urban Affairs*, 9: 103–123. doi:10.1111/j.1467-9906.1987.tb00468.x.

Lipe, K. & Lipe, D. (2016). Living the consciousness: Navigating the academic pathway for our children and communities. *International Journal of Qualitative Studies in Education*, 30(1), 32–47. doi:10.1080/09518398.2016.1243270.

Lipman, P. (2011). *The new political economy of urban education: Neoliberalism, race, and the right to the city*. New York, NY: Routledge.

Love, B. (2017). A ratchet lens: Black queer youth, agency, hip hop, and the black ratchet imagination. *Educational Researcher*, 46(9), 539–547.

Luke, A. (2006). Teaching after the market: From commodity to cosmopolitan. In Weis, L., McCarthy, C., & Dimitriadis, G. (Eds.) *Ideology, curriculum, and the new sociology of education: Revisiting the work of Michael Apple*. New York: Routledge.

Madison, D. S. (2012). *Critical ethnography: Method, ethics, and performance*. Los Angeles, CA: Sage.

Madison, D.S. (2019). *Critical ethnography: Method, ethics, and performance*. Thousand Oaks, CA: Sage Publishing.

Malewski, E. (Ed.) (2010). *Curriculum studies handbook: The next moment*. New York: Routledge.

Marker, M. (2018). There is no place of nature; there is only the nature of place: Animate landscapes as methodology for inquiry in the Coast Salish territory. *International Journal of Qualitative Studies in Education*. doi:10.1080/09518398.2018.1430391

Marrun, N.A. (2018). The power of ethnic studies: portraits of first-generation Latina/o students carving out un sitio and claiming una lengua. *International Journal of Qualitative Studies in Education*, 31(4), 272–292. https://doi.org/10.1080/09518398.2017.1422288

Marston, S. A. (2000). The social construction of scale. *Progress in Human Geography* 24(2), 219–242.

Massey, D. (1978). Regionalism: Some current issues. *Capital & Class*, 2(3), 106–125. doi: 10.1177/030981687800600105.

Massey, D. (1994). *Space, place, and gender*. Minneapolis: University of Minnesota Press.

Massey, D. (1995). The conceptualization of place. In D. Massey & P. Jess (Eds.), *A place in the world?: Places, cultures, and globalization* (pp. 215–239). New York: Oxford University Press.

Massey, D. (2005). *For space*. London, UK: Sage.

Massey, D. & P. Jess (Eds). (1995). *A place in the world? Places, cultures, and globalization*. New York: Oxford University Press.

Massey, D.S., & Tannen, J. (2015). A research note on trends in Black hypersegregation. *Demography* 52, 1025–1034. doi: 10.1007/s13524-015-0381-6.

Mayo, C. (2017). Queer and trans youth: Relational subjectivity, and uncertain possibilities: Challenging research in complicated contexts. *Educational Researcher*, 46(9), 530–538.

McCarty, T.L. (2018). Concluding commentary: Reimagining education research from indigenous elsewheres. *International Journal of Qualitative Studies in Education*, 31(3), 231–234.

McKinney, M. (2000). A place to learn: Teachers, students, and classroom spaces. Unpublished Dissertation, University of North Carolina-Chapel Hill.

McKittrick, K. (2006). *Demonic grounds: Black women and the cartographies of struggle*. Minneapolis: University of Minnesota Press.

McKittrick, K. (Ed.). (2015). *Sylvia Wynter: On being human as praxis*. Durham; London: Duke University Press. doi:10.2307/j.ctv11cw0rj.

McLaren, P. (1994). *Life in schools: An introduction to critical pedagogy in the foundations of education*, 2nd edition. White Plains, NY: Longman.

Miller, J. (2005). *Sounds of silence breaking: Women, autobiography, curriculum*. New York: Peter Lang.

Morgan, J. (2002). Constructing school geographies. In M. Smith (Ed.), *Teaching geography in secondary schools: A reader* (pp. 40–59). London: Routledge/The Open University Press.

Mulcahy. D. (2012) Affective assemblages: body matters in the pedagogic practices of contemporary school classrooms, *Pedagogy, Culture & Society*, 20(1), 9–27. DOI: 10.1080/14681366.2012.649413

Nakagawa, Y. & Payne, P.G. (2016). Educational experiences of post-critical non-place. *International Journal of Qualitative Studies in Education*, 30(2), 147–160. doi:10.1080/09 518398.2016.1242802.

National Academies of Sciences, Engineering, and Medicine (NASEM) (2018). *Protecting the Health and Well-Being of Communities in a Changing Climate: Proceedings of a Workshop*. Washington, DC: The National Academies Press. https://doi.org/10.17226/24846.

Nespor, J. (1997). *Tangled up in school: Politics, space, bodies, and signs in educational process*. Mahwah, NJ: Lawrence Erlbaum Associates.

Nguyen, N., Cohen, D., Huff, A. (2017). Catching the bus: A call for critical geographies of education. *Geography Compass*, 11(8), 1–13. doi: 10.1111/gec3.12323.

Nieto, S. (1999). *The light in their eyes: Creating multicultural learning communities*. New York: Teachers College Press.

Noblit, G. (1999). The possibilities of postcritical ethnographies: An introduction to the issue, *Educational Foundations* 13(1), pp. 3–6.

Noblit, G. (2004). Reinscribing critique in educational ethnography: critical and postcritical ethnography. In K. B. deMarrais & S. D. Lapan (Eds.) *Foundations of research: methods of inquiry in education and the social sciences*. Mahwaw, NJ: Lawrence Erlbaum

Noblit, G. W., Flores, S. Y. & Murillo, E. G. (2004). Postcritical ethnography: An introduction. In G. W. Noblit, S. Y. Flores & E. G. Murillo, (Eds.), *Postcritical ethnography: Reinscribing critique* (pp. 1–52). Cresskill, NJ: Hampton.

Nxumalo, F. (2016). Towards 'refiguring presences' as an anti-colonial orientation to research in early childhood studies. *International Journal of Qualitative Studies in Education*, 29(5), 640–654. doi: 10.1080/09518398.2016.1139212.

O'Brian, L. M. (2000). 'Thinking about what we're doing' teaching foundations of education: Doing philosophy an building a course (with apologies to Maxine Greene). *Educational Foundations* 14(3): pp. 21–38.

Owens, D. (2001). *Composition and sustainability: Teaching for a threatened generation*. Urbana, IL: National Council of Teachers of English Press (Refiguring English Studies series).

Pickles, J. (2004). *A history of spaces: Cartographic reason, mapping and the geo-coded world*. New York: Routledge.

Pierce, R.B. (2005). *Polite protest: The political economy of race in Indianapolis, 1920-1970*. Bloomington, IN: Indiana University Press.

Pinar, W.F. (2003). *Handbook of international research in curriculum*. Mahwah, NJ: Lawrence Erlbaum.

Pinar, W. (2004) *What is curriculum theory?* Mahwah, NJ: Lawrence Erlbaum Associates.

Pinar, W.F. (2006). *The synoptic text today and other essays: Curriculum development after the Reconceptualization*. New York: Peter Lang.

Pinar, W.F., Reynolds, W.M., Slattery, P., & Taubman, P. (1995). *Understanding curriculum*. New York: Peter Lang.

Pope, D.C. (2001). *Doing school: How we creating a generation of stressed-out, materialistic, and miseducated students*. New Haven, CN: Yale University Press.

Price, J. N. (2001). Action research pedagogy and change. *Journal of Curriculum Studies*, 33(1): 43–77.

Quantz, R. (1992). On critical ethnography. In M. D. LeCompte, Millroy, W.L., & J. Preissle (Eds.), *The Handbook of Qualitative Research in Education*. San Diego: Academic Press, pp. 447–505.

Reynolds, M. (1998). The challenge of racial equality. In W. J. Reese (Ed.), *Hoosier schools: Past and present* (pp. 173–193). Bloomington, IN: Indiana University Press.

Roberts, M. (2000). The role of research in supporting teaching and learning. In Kent, A., (Ed.). *Reflective practice in geography teaching*, (pp. 287–296). Thousand Oaks, CA: Paul Chapman Publishing.

Rogers, D.L., Noblit, G.W. & P. Ferrel (1999). Action research as an agent for developing teachers' communicative competence. In Noblit, G.W. *Particularities: Collected essays on ethnography and education*. (pp.81–92). New York: Peter Lang.

Rose, G. (1997). Performing inoperative community, power, and change: The space and the resistance of some community arts projects. In Keith, M. & Pile, S. (Eds.) *Geographies of resistance*. London: Routledge.

Rothstein, R. (2017). *The color of law: A forgotten history of how our government segregated America*. New York: Liveright Publishing.

Said, E. (1978). *Orientalism*. New York: Random House.

Said, E. (1993). *Culture and Imperialism*. London. Chatto & Windus Ltd

Sassen, S. (2010). The city: Its return as a lens for social theory. *City, culture, and society*, 1(1), 3–11.

Sassen, S. (2011). *The city: Its return as a lens into larger economic and technological histories*. Retrieved August 15, 2016 from http://www.eera-ecer.de/ecer2011/programme/keynotespeakers/saskia-sassen/

Sassen, S. (2014). *Expulsions: Brutality and complexity in the global economy*. Cambridge, MA: Belknap Press.

Schmidt, S.J. (2010). Bringing the Other closer to home: Geography education in the post-colonial. *Critical Literacy: Theories and Practices*, 4(1), 29–47.

Schmidt, S.J. (2011). Theorizing place: Students' navigation of place outside the classroom. *Journal of Curriculum Theorizing*, 27(1), 20–35.

Schmidt, S.J. (2015). A queer arrangement of school: Using spatiality to understand inequity. *Journal of Curriculum Studies* 47(2), 253–273.

Schmidt, S. J., & Kenreich, T. W. (2015). In a space but not of it: Uncovering racial narratives through geography. In P. T. Chandler (Ed.), *Doing race in social studies: Critical perspectives*, (pp. 229–252). Charlotte, NC: Information Age Press.

Segall, A. & Helfenbein, R. (2008). Research on K-12 geography education. In L. Levstik & C. Tyson (Eds.) *Handbook of research in social studies education* (pp. 259–283). New York: Routledge.

Slater, F. (2001). Values and values education in the geography curriculum in relation to concepts of citizenship. In D. Lambert & P. Machon (Eds.), *Citizenship through secondary geography* (pp. 42–67). London and New York: Routledge.

Sobel, D. (1998). *Mapmaking with children: Sense of place education for the elementary years.* New York: Heinemann.

Soja, E.W. (1980). The socio-spatial dialectic. *Annals of the American Association of Geographers* 70(2), 207–225.

Soja, E. W. (1989). *Postmodern geographies: The reassertion of space in critical social theory.* New York, NY: Verso.

Soja, E. W. (1996). *Thirdspace: Journeys to Los Angeles and other real-and-imagined places.* Oxford: Blackwell.

Soja, E. (2010). *Seeking spatial justice.* Minneapolis: University of Minnesota Press.

Somerville, M. (2014). The power of place. In Steinberg, S. & Cannela, G. (Eds.). *Critical Qualitative research reader.* New York: Peter Lang, 67–81.

Spencer, H. (1859). *Education: Intellectual, moral, and physical.* New York: WM L Allison Company.

Stake, R. (1995). *The art of case study research.* Thousand Oaks, CA: Sage Publications.

Steinberg, S.R. & Kincheloe, J. (Eds.). (1997). *Kinderculture: The corporate construction of childhood.* Boulder, CO: Westview Press.

Summer, B.T. (2019). *Black in place: The spatial aesthetics of race in a post-chocolate city.* Chapel Hill: University of North Carolina Press. doi:10.5149/9781469654034_summers.

Tate, W. F. (2008). "Geography of opportunity": Poverty, place, and educational outcomes. *Educational Researcher, 37*(7), 397–411.

Taylor, H. (2005). *Gimme some space: How composition can benefit from critical geography.* Unpublished paper presented at the *Annual Meeting of the American Association for the Advancement of Curriculum Studies,* Montreal, Canada.

Taylor, C. M. (2007). Geographical information systems (GIS) and school choice: The use of spatial research tools in studying educational policy. In Gulson, K. N., Symes, C. (Eds.), *Spatial theories of education: Policy and geography matters* (pp. 77–93). New York: Routledge.

Thornton, S. J. (2003). *"Placing geography: Moving beyond the past in social studies education."* Paper presented at the *Annual meeting of the National Council for the Social Studies,* Chicago.

Tierney, W.G. & Ward, J.D. (2017). Coming out and leaving home: A policy and research agenda for LGBT youth homeless students. *Educational Researcher, 46*(9), 498–507.

Tsing, A.L. (1994). From the margins. *Cultural Anthropology* 9(3), 279–297.

Tsing, A. L. (2005). *Friction: An ethnography of global connection.* Princeton, NJ: Princeton University Press.

Tsing, A. L. (2012). On nonscalability: The living world is not amenable to precision-nested scales. *Common Knowledge* 18(3), 505–525. DOI: 10.1215/0961754X-1630424

Tsing, A. L. (2015). *The mushroom at the end of the world: On the possibility of life in capitalist ruins.* Princeton, NJ: Princeton University Press.

Tuan, Y. (1977). *Space and place: The perspective of experience.* Minneapolis, MN: University of Minnesota Press.

Tyack, D. & Cuban, L. (1995). *Tinkering toward utopia: A century of public school reform.* Cambridge, MA: Harvard University Press.

Valentine, G., Skelton, T., & Chambers, D. (1998). Cool places: An introduction to youth and youth cultures. In T. Skelton & G. Valentine (Eds.), *Cool places: Geographies of youth cultures*. New York: Routledge.

Valenzuela, A. (1999). *Subtractive schooling: U.S.-Mexican youth and the politics of caring*. New York: SUNY Press.

Waitoller, F.R. & Annamma, S.A. (2017). Taking a spatial turn in inclusive education. In M.T. Hughes & E. Talbott, (Eds.) *The Wiley Handbook of Diversity in Special Education*. doi:10.1002/9781118768778.ch2.

Wang, H. (2004). *The Call from the stranger on a journey home: Curriculum in third space*. New York: Peter Lang.

Warf, B. (1997) Teaching political economy and social theory in human geography, *Journal of Geography*, 96(2), 84–90. DOI: 10.1080/00221349708978765

Weedon, C. (1999). *Feminism, theory and the politics of difference*, Oxford, England: Blackwell.

Weheliye, A.G. (2014). *Habeus viscus: Racializing assemblages, biopolitics, and black feminist theories of the human*. Durham, NC: Duke University Press.

Willinsky, J. (1998). *Learning to divide the world: Education at empire's end*. Minneapolis: University of Minnesota Press.

Willis, P. (1977). *Learning to labor: How working class kids get working class jobs*. New York: Columbia University Press.

Wozolek, B. (2015). The presence of absence: The negotiation of space and place for students of color at a predominantly white suburban high school (Doctoral dissertation). Retrieved October 11, 2020 from http://rave.ohiolink.edu/etdc/view?acc_num=kent1436886233

Wozolek, B. (2018). In 1800 again: The sounds of students breaking. *Educational Studies: A Journal of the American Educational Studies Association*, 54(4), 367–381.

Wozolek, B. (2021). *Assemblages of violence in education: Everyday trajectories of oppression*. New York: Routledge.

Wynter, S. (1994). "No humans involved: An open letter to my colleagues." *Forum H.H.I Knowledge for the 21st Century* 1(1): 42–73.

Yon, D.A. (2000). *Elusive culture: Schooling, race, and identity in global times*. New York: SUNY Press.

Yoon, E.-S., & Lubienski, C. (2018). Thinking critically in space: Toward a mixed-methods geospatial approach to education policy analysis. *Educational Researcher*, 47(1), 53–61. https://doi.org/10.3102/0013189X17737284

INDEX